Making Mobilities Matter

I0123552

Making Mobilities Matter explores the interconnection between everyday practice and policy and planning in urban mobilities. It develops a theoretical framework for understanding everyday life and its mobilities in a mobile risk society and critiques the technocratic views that still dominate transport politics and research.

Recognizing the importance of culture and everyday life in shaping urban mobilities, it examines how contemporary communities exist, expand, and are sustained through localized and virtual forms of sharing responsibility, exchanging life experiences, creating meaning, and giving ontological security to people's lives. It also offers perspectives on the emotional aspect of mobilities in everyday life and how utopias can respond to these emotions. *Making Mobilities Matter* ends with a discussion of the prospects for urban mobilities in the future and how these issues are vital in battling climate change.

Making Mobilities Matter is an essential reading for students and researchers seeking to understand the importance of mobilities in sustainable urban development and tackling climate change.

Malene Freudendal-Pedersen is Professor in Urban Planning at Aalborg University, Denmark. Her research links sociology, geography, urban planning, and the sociology of technology. The mobilities turn has been significant and formative for her research focusing on mobilities practices, the interrelation between spatial and digital mobilities and its impacts on everyday life, cities, and societies. She is co-organizer of the Cosmobilities Network, co-founder and co-editor of the *Applied Mobilities* journal, and co-editor of the *Networked Urban Mobilities* book series (Routledge, 2017–).

Changing Mobilities

This series explores the transformations of society, politics and everyday experiences wrought by changing mobilities, and the power of mobilities research to inform constructive responses to these transformations. As a new mobile century is taking shape, international scholars explore motivations, experiences, insecurities, implications and limitations of mobile living, and opportunities and challenges for design in the broadest sense, from policy to urban planning, new media and technology design. With world citizens expected to travel 105 billion kilometres per year in 2050, it is critical to make mobilities research and design inform each other.
Series Editors: Monika Büscher, Peter Adey

Hybrid Mobilities
Transgressive Spatialities
Edited by Nadine Cattan and Laurent Faret

Making Mobilities Matter
Malene Freudendal-Pedersen

The Freedom Riders Across Borders
Contentious Mobilities
Barbara Lüthi

Alternative (Im)Mobilities
Edited by Maria Alice de Faria Nogueira

For a full list of titles in this series, please visit https://www.routledge.com/Changing-Mobilities/book-series/CHGMOB

'Mobilities matter! We all know this, but with Freudendal-Pedersen's new book we learn how profoundly this is the case. The book is sharp on the dilemmas and fragilities that everyday life mobilities lead to, and is illustrative to how small choices may have big effects. An important contribution to the mobilities literature on the edge of planetary challenge.'

Ole B. Jensen, *Deputy Director of Centre for Mobilities and Urban Studies (C-MUS), Aalborg University, Denmark*

'*Making Mobilities Matter* demonstrates why mobilities thinking is essential for addressing some of the biggest challenges of our time. Freudendal-Pedersen invites us to take seriously the richness and complexity of people's mobile lifeworlds that are insufficiently addressed by narrow economic or technocratic approaches to planning and design.'

David Bissell, *Associate Professor of Geography, The University of Melbourne, Australia*

'In clear-eyed and accessible prose *Making Mobilities Matter* invites us into the conversation on the connection between everyday mobilities and how we might find new pathways to achieve sustainable futures. Focusing on communities, meanings, and emotions, Freudendal-Pedersen's unique approach reminds us that we hold the future in our own hands. To change unsustainable mobilities requires that we reorganize everyday life, and that calls for alternative approaches toward future planning, in and with people. Through empirical research on mobilities practices and futures, this important book reveals a new paradigm in urban planning and changing mobilities.'

Mimi Sheller, *Dean of the Global School, Worcester Polytechnic Institute, USA*

Making Mobilities Matter

Malene Freudendal-Pedersen

Routledge
Taylor & Francis Group

LONDON AND NEW YORK

First published 2022
by Routledge
4 Park Square, Milton Park, Abingdon, Oxon OX14 4RN

and by Routledge
605 Third Avenue, New York, NY 10158

Routledge is an imprint of the Taylor & Francis Group, an Informa business

© 2022 Malene Freudendal-Pedersen

British Library Cataloguing-in-Publication Data
A catalogue record for this book is available from the British Library

Library of Congress Cataloging-in-Publication Data
Names: Freudendal-Pedersen, Malene, author.
Title: Making mobilities matter / Malene Freudendal-Pedersen.
Description: Abingdon, Oxon ; New York, NY : Routledge, 2022. | Series: Changing mobilities | Includes bibliographical references and index. | Identifiers: LCCN 2021058368 (print) | LCCN 2021058369 (ebook) | ISBN 9780367607883 (hardback) | ISBN 9780367607890 (paperback) | ISBN 9781003100515 (ebook) Subjects: LCSH: Urban transportation. | City planning. | Transportation--Planning. | Urban policy.
Classification: LCC HE305 .F748 2022 (print) | LCC HE305 (ebook) | DDC 388.4--dc23/eng/20211216
LC record available at https://lccn.loc.gov/2021058368
LC ebook record available at https://lccn.loc.gov/2021058369

ISBN: 9780367607883 (hbk)
ISBN: 9780367607890 (pbk)
ISBN: 9781003100515 (ebk)

DOI: 10.4324/9781003100515

Typeset in Times NR MT Pro
by KnowledgeWorks Global Ltd.

Contents

Acknowledgments

First, I want to thank the mobilities communities. This book developed by thinking together with engaged researchers and practitioners that have strived at developing an inclusive community for rethinking movement and its role in modern societies throughout two decades. The many articles that I encountered through my role as an editor for the journal *Applied Mobilities* and reviewer for the journal *Mobilities* have been a constant inspiration and helped broadening perspectives. This also applies for the edited books I, as well as others in the community, put together. They show the variety of ideas and attempts in Making Mobilities Matter. I also want to thank my research group Planning for Urban Sustainability, Department of Planning, Aalborg University, for their engagement and endeavors in creating sustainable futures.

This book only exists through the giving and inspiring work with great colleagues in a variety of research projects generously supported from: The Innovation Foundation Denmark (Sustainable Innovative Mobility Solutions); The Independent Research Fund Denmark (Urban Bicycle Mobilities and Mobility, Food and Housing in the Sustainable Transition of Everyday Life); EU, Jean Monnet Network, Erasmus+ (Cooperative, Connected and Automated Mobility: EU and Australasian Innovation); The Danish State Railways (Mobility in Daily Life – Between Freedom and Unfreedom); Roskilde University and Aalborg University (Mobilities Futures and the City).

Maja de Neergaard, Katrine Hartman-Petersen, and Sven Kesselring I owe a special thank for their critical and encouraging reading and co-thinking of the chapters in this book. It would not have become materialized without their support. Last, but not least, I want to thank my life essential friends, my amazing kids (the ones I made and the ones I have been allowed to borrow), and the love of my life who simply makes everything better.

1 Introduction

Everyday life is "puzzled" together by mobilities. Most of the time it is not a reflexive practice, it is just something we do on the phone, on the tablet, on the bike, in the bus, in the car, etc. We repeat it continuously every day, very often in more or less the same way and, as German sociologist Max Weber puts it, in a mental state *dull semi-consciousness*. There are routes and paths that we tap into without giving the mobilities much thought. What is important is what it enables us to do, this is what our minds are occupied with. Some years ago, I moved to a different part of Copenhagen, only about one kilometer from where I had previously lived. Some practices stayed the same, but I was surprised at how much reflexive energy I needed to put into moving between the different activities in my everyday life (such as taking the kids to school, work, grocery shopping). I often found myself on paths that were no longer the fastest, safest, or nicest way to go. My everyday mobilities routines were locked in and reformulating them required more energy than I had imagined. This might have been less obvious if I had moved to an entirely different area far away from my previous residence, but the shortness of the distance made me realize how my body was engaging in one kind of mobilities and allowing my mind to practice another.

The key point here is: everyday mobilities are routinized practices. In order to make everyday life work, there is no room for being reflexive on a daily basis on what is the cheapest, most sustainable, most practical, or fastest way to move between activities. Take morning routines as an example: the sequence of taking a shower, brushing teeth, eating breakfast, and having coffee is not renegotiated every morning. The same goes for mobilities. Living a late modern everyday life with all its (ostensible) opportunities for individuals to pursue in order to create the good life for themselves and their close ones is highly dependent on mobilities. In 2016, the EU's transport energy consumption was

DOI: 10.4324/9781003100515-1

34% higher than in 1990, and road transport had the largest growth, reflecting a decrease in the overall price of passenger cars (European Environment Agency, 2018). There is no way around the dominant role the private car has come to play in everyday mobilities and an "autologic" dominates today's civil society. In his book *Mobilities*, John Urry (2007, p. 130) goes as far as to suggest that "civil society in most countries should now be re-conceptualized as a civil society of 'car-drivers' and 'car-passengers'." The rise in automobility in relation to the climate change agenda is creating conflicts in everyday life which is termed as the "mobile risk society" (Kesselring, 2008a) and produces ambivalences. In the mobile risk society, individuals are themselves responsible for choosing the "right" trajectories and design the good life for themselves and their families. Modern institutions expect that individuals can overlook the full complexity of living in a reflexive modern society even if they know this is not possible. Thereby responding to issues such as climate change and automobility are individualized and often involve either ignoring the problems or feeling apathetic about changing everyday practices. Understanding the routinized everyday mobilities is the starting point for thinking about how to initiate change toward more sustainable mobilities. In this book, main focus is on the empirical field of everyday mobilities, with a primary focus on physical mobilities such as cars, trains, and cycles. But everyday mobilities also mean policy and planning when these scales are inextricably linked.

The interconnection between everyday practice and policy and planning is essential in battling climate change. This is not a new thing, not least in relation to one of the core issues: transportation. Already in the UN's 1992 blueprint for Agenda 21 from the Rio Summit, transport was outlined as an important focus area and has since been a recurring issue in national and international politics. To mention just two examples: the report *Mobility 2030: Meeting the Challenges to Sustainability*, published by the World Business Council for Sustainable Development in 2004, highlights the fact that no one-best-way solution exists and broad engagement and collaboration is needed (World Business Counsil for Sustainable Development, 2004). Most recently, the Sustainable Development Goals have highlighted the need for sustainable mobility with a focus on the Avoid-Shift-Improve approach to "promote ... multimodal, collective-shared mobility solutions" (High-level Advisory Group on Sustainable Transport, 2016, p. 7). Thus it is not knowledge on possible ways to change the current system, that is missing. The issue here is the isolated view on the transportation system that fails to realize how mobilities are much more than getting efficiently from A to B. *Making Mobilities Matter* contributes to the agenda of strengthening the impact of mobilities research in urban planning. Despite a growing focus on transportation's impact on climate change as well as an increasing emphasis on designing cities for people, a traditional approach to transportation still dominates urban planning and policy. Engaging with the mobilities of everyday life can help to understand the need for a broader and more inclusive approach, or, more precisely, to better understand "the culture of mobilities." With mobilities, the perspective changes and new pathways to achieving sustainable futures open up.

The mobilities paradigm is occupied with understanding large-scale and local processes related to daily movements of people, goods, capital, and information (Adey et al., 2014; Cresswell, 2006; Urry, 2007). Using the term "mobilities" instead of "mobility" emphasizes how different forms of movement, whether physical or virtual, are interconnected and produce and reproduce each other. When driving a car for instance, the navigation system or the radio are other mobilities interacting with the driving, not to mention the whole infrastructural, economic, and emotional system supporting the practice. In this way, the concept of mobilities is made as a plural word exactly to highlight that which surrounds and supports, for instance, driving. Mobilities have a visible imprint on the city, especially automobility with its domination of city space determining which spaces can be lived spaces. Cities and regions are comprised of social, technological, geographic, cultural, and digital mobilities networks, and through these they are linked to the global "network society." The inseparable bonds between cities and mobilities have developed over time, and our future cities will be shaped even more by the mobilities of people, goods, transport, waste, information, data, and signs (Ritzer, 2010; Urry, 2007). Via a number of significant technological developments in transportation and communication, cities have changed their pulse, pace, and reach. People increasingly assume that holidays are spent far away from the locality of everyday lives. Work life has become highly dependent on virtual interactions. Instead of a following decline in physical mobilities, virtual mobilities have made new connections possible and face-to-face meetings are still seen as required for trustworthy business relationships. Virtual mobilities in the form of smartphones, iPads, and computers play a determining role in everyday life choices, chores, and practices. In this sense, there is no doubt that the technologies, especially those that support our virtual mobilities, have changed, and today technology is something no one can escape. In his last book, *The Metamorphoses of the World* (2016), Ulrich Beck points out that even if we do not use or have access to iPads, smartphones, computers, or travel, we still live in a world that is centered around mobilities that have an impact on our lives. The mobile global economic markets are influencing housing prices, news stories, food, and all the other elements that are shaping our emotional and material lives.

Despite this, it seems that within the contexts of urban planning, transport engineering, and economic politics, contemporary discourses of planning and designing mobilities have dealt with the issue of traffic as an isolated issue (Jensen and Richardson, 2003). Within this tradition, the questions of "why" and "for what and whom" often seem to be missing. For most cities, this results in a prioritization of the automobile systems. This is counterproductive to a sustainability agenda in that it intensifies and accelerates climate change, creates traffic jams due to induced traffic, and continues the ongoing destruction of public spaces (Newman and Kenworthy, 2015). In this sense, modern planning paradigms are still "technocentric" with an ideal of flow and "zero friction" (Hajer, 1999). The dominating neoliberal concept of an economy based on global flows of trade and workforce (Larner, 2000; Tickell and Peck, 2002) results in an unchallenged principle of "seamless mobility" as the pathway for the efficient organization of cities. As Urry (2007, p. 20) puts it: "There is too much transport in the study of travel and not enough society and thinking through the complex intersecting relations between society and transport." In addition, the system of automobility, and its efficiency and benefits, is often overestimated (Rode et al., 2015). This perpetuates the perception of the car as a mobility artifact without serious alternatives.

In line with the technocentric paradigm, the "sustainable" solution to this is the automatized vehicle. On several occasions, I have heard traffic planners and politicians talk about the future of automatized driving with the vision that in the future you "curl up in your car with your comforter and coffee and get a couple more hours of sleep while being transported to work." The snappy answer I have given in these situations is that in the future "I still want to wake up in the morning, cuddle with my partner for a few minutes before I go in and kiss the kids good morning, and then have breakfast together." From a technocentric perspective, the automatized car provides new, fantastic opportunities; it works in exactly the same way as an ordinary car except that transport time can become *productive* time. Based strictly on a narrow economic perspective, this is meaningful in terms of an idea of more work produced, better surplus for the company, and more taxes paid; however, in a broader perspective, it contains numerous economic, cultural, social, and environmental elements that are destructive for cities. In order to have fully automatized cars that glide effortlessly from place to place, pathways need to be emptied of unregulated movement—even more so than today. The livable city, which is essential in the global city competition, is not that systematized, at least not when you look at the Forbes list of the most livable cities in the world. Also, in the technocentric rush of the possibilities the automatized car entails, the most mundane everyday practices, that are a big part of creating meaning in everyday lives, are forgotten. This path-dependent way of thinking about cities' mobilities seems widely unchallenged, indicating the need for a new level of reflexivity on how to make cities livable places for the good mobile life, environments of justice, equality, and access to common goods (Sheller, 2018), a need for a subject-oriented turn in urban planning and design (Schmalz-Bruns, 1995) that considers sustainability and socially cohesive cities as *essential* and not just "nice-to-have" features. Nigel Thrift (2001, p. 48) talks about "an emancipatory politics of bare life" among other things, including contemplation. This idea can be translated into thinking about cities created around the needs of walkers (bodies), instead of creating an architecture of automobility (metal boxes). In line with this Peñalosa (2008, p. 319) states that: "So far, urban quality of life has been referred to in relation to issues such as equality and happiness. But there is another aspect to consider—a country's competitiveness in the information age will depend largely on the quality of life in its cities."

In the last 100 years, many cities have been designed with the needs of cars as a prerequisite because the car played a significant role in the move from the first to the second modernity. On an everyday scale, this meant the opportunity to leave the locked-in life in traditional communities where tradition (and physical proximity) determined life courses. With extensive opportunities for virtual and physical mobilities, not least the car, individualization became a keyword within social science, followed by warnings of risks of anonymity and anomie. This became a story about the erosion of communities and a weakening of social ties. It has been argued that close communities have all but disappeared and are no longer meaningful; in this book, however, I argue that they have not lost their meaning and significance. Changing everyday mobilities practices means changing the organization of everyday life. Everyday life organization is also about creating ontological security, to have meaning and get recognition for the paths chosen. This happens in communities and during the last decade, communities have re-emerged as one of the important issues within public debate and political discussions as constituting the backbone of cities. Communities can emerge simply because people are continuously looking for other beings or objects to make sense of, or create meaning around, dynamics that are transforming their lived experiences (Dewey, 1954; Lippmann, 1993/1927). New communities may take many unexpected shapes, and by moving beyond localized communities by means of virtual communities, the sense of belonging to a community might find new ways of establishing ideas of common sensitivity toward family life, neighborhoods, democracy, working life, or global issues (Delanty, 2003; Wellman and Gulia, 1999). Virtual and physical mobilities simultaneously affect local and global communities by opening up different arenas for co-existence. Globalization is a process penetrating cities and transforming internal dynamics by inserting people, objects, and information from all over the world into the localized space. Globalization has the potential to both rupture existing links and create new ones in people's everyday experiences. Furthermore, communities and social ties are still found where they were thought to have been largely eroded by mobility, instability, and fluidity.

Thus, communities are still very much there as a precondition for lived lives, and it is therefore pertinent to consider them fully when working with future cities. The encompassing mobilities dominating modern lives mean that we need to move beyond an understanding of communities only as localized (spatial) fixities and investigate communities on the move. This is not a new approach. Several scholars within social science and mobilities research have used many different approaches to describe social interactions, for example, networks or assemblages. In this book, I return to the concept of communities because of the emotional aspects within this approach. Community captures essential emotions and plays a significant role in the making of meaning in everyday life, an understanding of which is essential if we wish to create sustainable urban mobilities in the future. Using examples from previous qualitative empirical work I did on issues surrounding mobilities, I argue in this book that communities still provide essential ontological security to everyday lives and, as such, communities have the power to change practices. The examples used in this book come from two ongoing and three previous research projects centered around mobilities practices and futures. Even if communities did not constitute the main focus of this research, they, however, always appeared in the periphery. In this way, this book is also an explorative process outlining a pathway to explore the role and significance of communities and emotions in mobile everyday lives.

Today, it seems the power of individualization as the pathway to freedom has eclipsed the power of people, communities, and institutions as the drivers of change. As a consequence, lived lives are often given little significance in relation to change as people are only seen as individualized consumers. There is no doubt that modes of thought and possibilities in everyday life are influenced and guided to a great extent by the capitalist system. Lived lives have different expressions, also decided by factors such as class, gender, education, and location. These factors aside, however, the values, emotions, and dreams of everyday life are something most have in common. Behind the individualized, there is still a need for an ontological security based on wants and desires, security, safety, and communities. These emotions are ascribing significant meaning to elements of everyday life and are an important driver for change. Utopias are, so to speak, a visualization of these emotions. They tell us something about what matters to us and what we don't like. However, using dreams, utopias, and imagination to inhabit the kind of world we want endangers the fragile irrationalities holding everyday life together, but without imagination and aspiration, another more real and significant menace is born when these imaginings, dreams, and utopias disappear, and we then subsequently forget how to play and live life beyond the framework that already exist.

Everyday life is both practical as well as influenced by conceptions of time, freedom, and community. Sharing responsibilities, exchange of life experiences, continuity and meaning, and ontological security is essential elements of communities, and they are based on emotions. Emotions are embedded in the mobilities ontology, and research on "affective mobilities" has shown the importance of what happens to the bodies on the move and bodies settling down and building a sense of home and belonging (Glaveanu and Womersley, 2021, p. 2). Mobilities research has developed an understanding of embodied and sensory experiences as essential in shaping the institutional material arrangements and practices of mobilities. The emotional forces of experiences on the move, how to connect everyday life so that needs are meet as much as possible, the freedom, the flexibility, the communities, the activities, are about emotions. Nobody wants to just go from A to B, there is a reason to move and there is a reason to arrive. It is what comes before and after (and don't forget the time spent moving) that matters to people. By discharging emotions, possibilities for change are not revealed.

For emotions to become powerful and included in visions and policies, "collaborative storytelling" plays a key role. James Throgmorton and Leonie Sandercock (2003) frame this necessity by stating that stories have a fundamental "persuasive character" when it comes to making decisions on the future of cities. These stories resonate with everyday life and its ethics, morals, hopes, and dreams and are a pathway to regulate or encourage people to change practices. In my previous work, I have captured this through the concept of "structural stories" (Freudendal-Pedersen, 2015, 2009) based on Giddens' theory of structuration. Structural stories, such as "if you have kids, you need a car," are somehow at the bottom of all path dependencies, including the replication and iteration of these stories that constitute realities and "normalities" today (see Birtchnell, 2016). In this sense, the story of the automatized (private) car fits perfectly into these structural stories, and the question "is this a city we would like to live in?" fades away. Taking a more subject-oriented approach to city planning might entail insisting on automatization and sharing as inseparable concepts. This requires an understanding of how communities, as essential parts of mobile lives, can help to create future cities for people. Communities entail emotions and meaning, and it is vital to pay appropriate attention to them because of their interconnections with mobilities and materialities in the city and hopeful possible futures present in people's lives. Bauman (2009, p. 30) refers to the power of emotions in discussing why Václav Havel left such a powerful imprint on the world:

> He had only three weapons: hope, courage, and stubbornness. These are primitive weapons, nothing high-tech about them. And they are the most mundane, common weapons: humans all have them (...) Only we use them much too seldom.

Using emotions and utopias in re-thinking urban mobilities *IN* and *WITH* society provides an alternative approach toward future planning.

An increased focus on the "Human Scale" is essential, not least if Jeremy Rifkin is correct in his prediction that a massive change is coming in the future, spurred largely by economic initiatives based on sharing. In his (2000) bestseller *The Age of Access*, he claimed that future societies will not be organized around individual ownership; instead, new collective forms of consumption and sharing will play a central role in the organization of everyday life, the business world, and the economy. We can already see many of these initiatives blooming in relation to for instance Mobility as a Service (MaaS) present in many future urban plans. Despite these future visions, restrictions on car ownership and driving are still unthinkable for many politicians and transport planners. Instead, an agenda focusing on creating urban spaces where living, moving, and dwelling are in the center is often more acceptable. These plans entail restrictions on car driving and ownership but focus on creating livable green cities with active green mobilities and their implementation in different urban areas has so far been a very successful strategy to limit the impact from automobility. The projects create common future stories about the quality of the urban. This agenda has very much been promoted though "tactical urbanism" (Lydon and Garcia, 2015), where the redevelopment is framed as test scenarios using prototyping in the form of colors on the road, flowerpots, and benches. This approach makes it possible to rapidly make tangible what seem purely abstract and thereby enable a comprehension of the change in its context and complexity.

The main point here is to remember to ask the right questions and not only present glossy solutions when it is unclear what the roots of the problems are. This is also very important in relation to planning for smart cities which often is presented cleansed of human interactions. Instead it focuses on order and cleanliness of the everyday that has little to do with emotional and messy everyday life practices. A smart sustainable mobilities culture is about more than technology and needs an understanding of everyday movement as much more than speed, efficiency, and accessibility. Mobilities research can contribute to the sustain(ability) and the response(ability) in relation to climate change and make it a keyword in mobility and planning. The response-ability can only be created when there is respect and open-mindedness towards what matters to people and need a conscious approach to one's own ethics and one's own ontology (Freudendal-Pedersen, 2014b). With the significant role of the empirical within mobilities research mobile methods provide the opportunity to develop new critical engagements with the future (Urry and Büscher, 2009). This entails the questions "why," "for what," and "for whom" as a pathway to develop alternatives to the dominating technocratic view on future urban mobilities where transdiciplinarity, with other research disciplines, stakeholders, and citizens, is a key element.

Making Mobilities Matter has an outset in the urban which represents a scale of societal organization well suited to addressing the issue of sustainable mobilities. It is in cities that the problems with extensive car use are most visible in terms of congestion, noise, pollution, and occupation of city space, and it is in cities that public transport, cycling, walking, and diverse sharing solutions are most present. Cities set the standards for national and international politics in relation to mobilities. However, the fact that it *is* on a city scale does not necessarily mean that it is *not* on a rural scale. I would argue that the contents of this book are also relevant to rural areas: the opportunities for change might be more limited due to the availability of alternatives, but the understanding of everyday life mobilities, communities, and emotions as a driver for change is equally relevant. Similarly, while the book *is* written from a Global North perspective, this does not imply that it is *not* relevant to the Global South. The affluent middle class dominates politics and planning in the Global North, even more so in the Scandinavian welfare states. They also dominate the agenda in international politics and demonstrate a hierarchy of rights based on mode of movement. When Peñalosa (2008), with the Global South as point of departure, claims that governments have, to the highest degree, failed to comply with democratic principles in relation to transport, this is also very relevant in the Global North.

> ...the most sustainable city is, before anything else, the one most propitious to human happiness. And although human happiness has many definitions and requirements, in terms of habitat it demands elements such as being able to walk and play; having contact with nature such as found in parks, trails and waterfronts; being able to see and be with people; and feeling included and not inferior (Peñalosa, 2008, p. 319).

I am not arguing that essential differences do not exist between the institutional material arrangements in the Global South and the Global North. To give just one significant difference, women in Denmark are not avoiding public transport due to the fear of sexual harassment. My point is that paying attention to the issues this book focuses on is equally important everywhere, even if contexts and expression differ.

The book is divided into six chapters covering both the institutional material arrangements surrounding everyday mobilities and the practical and emotional aspects. After the introduction Chapter 2, *Voicing everyday life*, unfolds the theoretical framework for understanding everyday life and its mobilities. The mobile risk society (Kesselring, 2008a) where environmental, economic, and social risks are increasingly crucial to the social structures of societies forms the starting point for understanding contemporary mobile everyday life. The quantity of risks has not increased in modern societies; what has increased due to mobilities is our knowledge of risks and their consequences (Beck, 1992). Instant communication means an overload of information about global events and new knowledge (time-space compression); therefore, everyday life today means living with reflexivity and time pressure as a constant component and thus a lot of choices made possible by mobilities. As the traditions of premodern society are no longer available, people are required to constantly reflect upon which kind of life to lead and what practices to maintain To handle this and the ambivalences that come along with knowing and not knowing, individuals chose a lifestyle, often with certain mobilities practices embedded.

To understand how these practices are embedded and argued as structural stories, the focus is on "individuals-in-relations" as that which constitutes certain rationalities about mobilities practices. Berger and Luckmann (1966) describe the institutionalization and creation of knowledge engendered in a continuous construction where different actors characterize mutually habitual actions. This concept of institutions holds both the structure and system (in Giddens' 1984 terminology) in a process of structuration where human action simultaneously structures and *is* structured by society. Thus changing practices lies in changing the larger stories to guide the everyday practice of "individuals-in-relations" by questioning or re-conceptualizing the "normality" or "taken-for-granted naturalness" of specific practices.

This approach has been developed in an ongoing research process where the theoretical and the empirical are constantly informing and developing each other. The starting point for the research has been to give voice to the conflicting interpretations and practices of everyday life mobilities, the significance and meaning these mobilities have, and the city they are part of creating. The material from these research projects has formed the arguments and the thinking in this book, and Chapter 2 provides a short discussion of the different methodologies facilitating this research. To end the chapter, four research projects from which examples are used throughout the book are briefly mentioned. The book does not describe these projects in detail to build an empirical argument, but references will be provided for those interested in diving into the empirical work.

In Chapter 3, *Planning for technology or people—the human scale*, the technocratic starting point that still dominates transport politics and research will be discussed. The transdisciplinary mobilities research will be used as an entry point to open up new understandings of the interconnectedness between the city, its mobilities, and the people using them. The chapter begins by going through some of the concepts within transport and mobilities that are crucial to understanding the institutional material arrangements framing mobilities. This chapter focuses on traffic and transportation and all its practicalities and traditions to unfold the differences between these approaches and the mobilities paradigm. Whereas traffic and transport are seen as closed systems in the city, mobilities research holds an understanding that cities are shaped by the mobilities that support and develop modern lives within them. Today's cities are composed of complex settings of social, technological, geographical, cultural, and digital networks of mobilities (Graham and Marvin, 2002; Sheller and Urry, 2006). This interdependence has developed over time, through a series of large-scale technological transitions in transport and communications. Due to this, cities have changed rhythm, speed, and reach. Understanding the flow in cities purely as individual choices, technological transformations, or economic forces overlooks the fact that practices and networks are culturally assembled when producing and performing city space (Jensen, 2014).

Today, cities are nodes in global networks and "The Urban Age" (Burdett, 2010) connects urban spaces in a global pattern and structure. This keeps cities, with their institutions, actors, and forms of life, in the global "space of flows" but is also changing and threatening the very nature of what we used to consider the urban form or fabric. Time-space compression, the digitization of the world, and the ongoing individualization process have a deep impact on all spheres of life. Thus, in the Urban Age, the future of urban mobilities has become a key topic. The question of how to structure existing and future cities and the *scapes* of cities is also a question of how to "design" social layout and human interactions (Jensen, 2013; Latour, 1991). The technocratic starting point that dominates ideas of future cities tends to focus on the technological feasibility and legitimacy of measures, based on existing data, models, and calculations. However, the most important questions—why, for what, and for whom?—are not present. The absence of these important questions does not, however, work well in relation to the global city competition where politicians, planners, and architects compete in creating communities within livable cities. This constitutes an interesting dilemma, and resolving this requires an increased focus on the emotional aspects and practices of communities.

Chapter 4, *Communities on the move*, looks at how contemporary communities exist, expand, and are sustained through localized and virtual forms of sharing responsibility, exchanging life experiences, creating meaning, and giving ontological security to people's lives.

Understanding community and the influence mobility has on its maintenance or erosion due to increased individualism has a long scholarly tradition (Bauman, 2001; Putnam, 2000; Tönnies, 1957). Tönnies' conceptualized *Gemeinschaft*—a community with social interactions—as constituted through village cultures, common religious practice, and family life with all its unquestioned tradition.

He distinguished it from *Gesellschaft*—society with indirect interactions—as constituted through the industrial society where human interactions were loose and regulated through contracts and exchange of capital. This understanding of a community as something that "just is" is what makes Bauman, 44 years later, state that communities are an image of a world that we no longer have access to. In the same book, Bauman (2001, p. 39) also argues that communities are necessary for humanity's existence and continuation. The need for communities seems to be omnipresent because they offer ontological security by generating feelings of acceptance and mutual assistance.

Through examples from previous research, I show how modern, live communities still rely upon the need for exchanging everyday experiences and sharing responsibilities. The different forms of presence, commitment, and intentionality are simultaneously localized and continued at a distance, through physical and virtual mobilities. Individuals are continuously seeking out new communities that offer many of the very same elements as traditional communities did, be that local communities, virtual communities, or hybrid communities.

The networked mobilities transforming modern lives through diverse technologies that manage communication, transportation, and also relationships of various kinds are often associated with a loss of the communities which are the source of stability, coherence, and embeddedness. The routines of everyday life (associated with, for example, kids, home-making, friends, and leisure activities) continue to generate the meaning-making and ontological security conventionally associated with notions of community. The small groups through which these routines are practiced are communities, which provide contemporary "frames" within which life experiences can be exchanged, and according to which late-modern subjectivities are shaped (Bauman, 2001; Giddens, 1991). Today, communities exist through places as well as their intersecting routes (Ingold, 2007). In a mobile world, community-forming practices of interaction and responsibility sharing often rely less on the spatial (e.g., relationship courses, Facebook groups, diverse radio programs on childcare), even as neighborhood-oriented interactions remain significant to individuals' understanding of the "good life" (e.g., soccer clubs or dinner clubs, neighbors commuting together on bikes, trains, or in cars). Understanding communities within a mobile world needs to take this seriously: they are in *flow*, they *move*. A specific community may not last forever, but only for the short specific phase of a certain point in life—but it has meaning and it matters.

In Chapter 5, *Emotions and utopias*, the focus is on the emotional aspect of mobilities in everyday life, always present but often overlooked. Theoretical approaches that encompass the emotional and meaning-making aspects and the lay normativity always present when engaging with practice is essential. Everyday life is not an isolated unit but is constantly challenged and influenced by the multi-scale character of social practice, identity formation, global and local news, commercials, and politics. The basis on which people build their everyday lives reveals that which creates meaning and significance—in Sayer's words, *Why Things Matter to People* (Sayer, 2011)—and thus also how, through their practice, they shape societal institutions. Everyday life practices are about practical things but are also influenced by significant stories about and emotions related to time, freedom, and community.

These stories are given particular attention through the "argumentative turn" in policy analysis that through this investigates shifts in society's discursive patterns and structures (Fischer and Forester, 1993; Fischer and Gottweis, 2012). This starting point necessitates a subject-oriented approach in urban planning where sustainability and socially cohesive cities are essential, rather than "nice-to-have" features of a utopian post-materialist world. Communicative planning and storytelling offer the tools to understand the significance of creating new "utopias" about everyday life rhythms, hopes, dreams, and expectations (Freudendal-Pedersen and Kesselring, 2016; Sandercock, 2003). Even if these hopes and dreams are not the first thing the interviewees are talking about, showing an interest in their everyday life stories opens up many new orientations toward possible different futures (Kaplan and Ross, 1987). This is different from futuristic stories about the city, its everyday life, and its mobilities. Movies, books, and different futurologists extrapolating future lives most often describe a future where emotions are erased and irrelevant. Within city planning, the legacy of Marinetti/Futurism and Le Corbusier are often used as examples of misanthropic city planning, but their utopias for future lives were an attempt to create the good life in the city. Utopias can provide orientations toward futures—orientations that are needed in order not to move forward following the same path.

Without utopias, rational starting points where emotions are understood as irrelevant and that fail to comprehend and understand what goes on, not only in the virtual but also the physical mobilities, will be sustained. If we start from the viewpoint that communities are disappearing, the emotions associated with ontological security and responsibility as drivers of change are lost. Most importantly, paying attention to emotions does not equal neglecting rationalities or systemic thinking. Through a shift in focus away from individuals as rational economic beings when deciding which mobilities to use in everyday life, perspectives on the emotionally driven practice of everyday life mobilities become visible. This creates a storytelling that responds to the needs and aspirations of citizens and politicians when suggesting alternative mobilities futures in the city.

In Chapter 6, *Futures*, different perspectives for the mobilities of future cities are discussed. We have never been more individualized in our way of being together, but, at the same time, we have never been more common in our ways of being individualized. If we look at the millennium generation, we see that they have a life on virtual platforms: sitting in their rooms at their computers or in public spaces on their smartphones. But what we also know is that they visit the same places; they have a community based around individualized experiences shared with friends and acquaintances. In his (2014) book *The Zero Marginal Cost Society*, Jeremy Rifkin writes about the eclipse of capitalism due to the growing interest in the sharing economy. He refers to a survey of 3,000 millennial consumers in the US (born between 1981 and 2000). When they were asked to list their 31 most preferred brands, the top ten mainly consisted of internet firms, and no car firms were present. Car technology, which, to a degree, has been seen as a major driving force in the erosion of communities, seems to have lost some of its importance. The car once functioned as a rite of transition, getting your driver's license at 18 (16 in some places), which led to adulthood, freedom, and interdependence. This no longer appears to be the case.

This, however, does not mean that young people are no longer interested in physical mobility, meeting people face to face, or visiting places. With time space compression the acceptance of covering miles to seek out opportunities and events has grown. The difference is that it seems the need to *own* the technology, is replaced with the need to *access* it. This brings MaaS in as a central player for future mobilities (Canzler and Knie, 2016). Planning cities with a focus on lived lives and access instead of ownership clashes with the "neotechnological automobilization" (Nixon, 2012) that is still the dominant response to energy use issues. Though "tactical urbanism" (Lydon and Garcia 2015), the redevelopment of urban space framed as test scenarios can challenge this and inform long-term implementations. Here visualizing proposals for plans and projects demands plays a big role, making it possible to show context, thereby creating very specific images and narratives. The main point here is to remember to ask the right questions and not only present glossy solutions when it is unclear what the roots of the problems are. The right questions need both an internal and external critique. This is also relevant in relation to smart cities that often becomes grounded in an engineering logic where the promise is an optimization of urban infrastructure and networks. Smart cities are also about human interactions and must be a system that is just and fair in the collection and distribution of data and does not favor specific forms of mobilities. Creating livable green cities might need transdisciplinary thoughtfully crafted visualizations can help imagining the *possible impossibles.* These utopian reflections carry the potential to break through the barriers of convention and create common stories as well as a response-ability toward sustainable mobilities futures.

2 Voicing everyday life

Everyday life is all around us; it is repeated, adjusted, and renewed as we go through different phases in life. Everyday life is producing and reproducing cultures, not least cultures of mobilities, and more or less sustainable activities are embedded here as practices that are taken for granted. The aim of this chapter is to give voice to these everyday activities, trivial though they may seem, and underline their significance, a significance that is even more pronounced when the issue is sustainable mobilities and the change of practice this entails. Later in this chapter, I elaborate on the perspective of changing everyday practices but let me be clear from the outset: change of practice is not just an individual issue. What is relevant here is *individuals-in-relations*, it is in the interactions that cultures are produced and reproduced. These interactions can be with other individuals or with the institutional material arrangements, where the making of meaning takes place.

Change in everyday life and practice is often labeled as a "soft" area where we need soft measures to change to soft modes of transport using soft methodologies. First of all, there is nothing as hard as culture, and second of all, the use of terms such as "hard" and "soft" methods/data/modes of transport needs to be replaced with content words (such as cycling, walking, interviews, focus groups, culture, and communication). Traditionally, what is often termed "hard" data is what forms the major platform for decisions in transport planning and policy, be they socioeconomic models, modeling of data sets, or technologies. Then, whatever has been termed "soft" is what comes after to regulate how humans react to or make use of specific technologies. There is an urgent need to rank soft or hard items alongside each other on an equal footing if any changes are to be made in the current unsustainable system of mobilities: the different types of knowledge and methodologies need to interact. This is not possible with the current power relationship that exists between hard and soft,

DOI: 10.4324/9781003100515-2

and yes, of course, it is gendered (Listerborn and Neergaard, 2021). It is not rocket science to replace these two words with content words. Let's not talk about soft modes of transport, let's talk about cycling, walking, and micro-mobilities; let's not talk about hard data, let's talk about modeling and statistics. I could go on at length but the main point here is that words matter, and it is about time to start over and recognize that the different elements of current mobilities cultures are equally important.

Henri Lefebvre in his 1947 book *Critique de la vie quotidienne* (translated into English in 1991 as "Critique of Everyday Life") blamed Marxists and Marxism as the reason why investigations of everyday life fall into the "less powerful" category. He stated that the downgrading of the importance of everyday life is due to the ever-present ambivalences or ambiguity that complicate the "simplicity" of capitalism and political economy: "*...ambiguity* is a category of everyday life, and perhaps an essential category. It never exhausts its reality: from the ambiguity of consciousnesses and situations spring forth actions, events, results, without warning" (Lefebvre, 1991a, p. 18). Lefebvre refers to Marx when pointing to the fact that accumulation and enjoyment as coexisting needs tear individuals apart and therefore: "...a distinction was made between man 'as man' one the one hand and the working man on the other (more clearly among the bourgeoisie, of course, than among the proletariat). Family life became separate from productive activity. And so did leisure" (Lefebvre, 1991a, p. 31). What Lefebvre is pointing to here is how the dominance of the capitalist system meant focusing on the individual as a productive entity with all the rationalities embedded therein. The ambiguity of everyday life and all its different rationalities made a clear system opaque, and as such, rejecting its importance became the solution. This is why the separation between working life and other life became the norm, as if stepping through the doorway of the workplace involved sloughing one's everyday skin. Everyday life, its culture, its morals, its ethics, is the full life: it consists of many different activities demanding different types of responses, but it is still the full life. The aim of this chapter is to underline the importance of understanding everyday life and the role it plays in changes toward sustainable mobilities. The increase in cars and trips has much to do with political economy (Conley and McLaren, 2012; Urry, 2004), but there is also a part that is about everyday life with all its emotions and feelings. This is because the car is so much more than just a technology that offers fast and flexible transportation. In an article in 2004, Mimi Sheller elaborates on this by saying that:

By taking seriously how people feel about and in cars, and how the feel of different car cultures elicits specific dispositions and ways of life, we will be in a better position to re-evaluate the ethical dimensions of car consumption and the moral economics of car use. Only then can we consider what will really be necessary to make the transition from today's car cultures (and the automotive emotions that sustain them) to more socially and environmentally 'responsible' transportation cultures (Sheller, 2004, pp. 4–5)

In this chapter. this emotional and routinized everyday life is in focus.

So what is the everyday?

For most people, everyday life is a patchwork of interconnected activities, meaning mobilities is an integrated part of everyday life. Many of its activities are routinized and, like specific early-morning routines, taken for granted. The entry point to everyday life in this book is not there to designate a distinct reality such as mobilities, the home, and online communities. Rather, everyday life is an epistemological starting point that entails a certain mode of thought in research and that offers a specific view on the politics and planning of mobilities, as Guillaume and Huysmans (2019, p. 281) point out:

> Everyday objects, practices and people as such are not the main stake of the game, however. They are tools that bring different conceptions of the international and political life, to bear upon scholarly work; conceptions that decenter how politics and political relevance is usually thought through in the relevant fields of study within which these everyday analyses situate themselves.

The everyday perspective is there as a certain starting point that provides access to understanding how specific practices are produced and reproduced, thus producing certain cultures that also produce and reproduce politics and planning in certain ways. In other words, the everyday cannot be detached from the institutional material arrangements that frame it. Everyday life shapes ethics, morals, and emotions that are carried through into whatever we do or wherever we do it. Lefebvre elegantly frames this when saying that: "...everyday life is the supreme court where wisdom, knowledge and power are brought to judgement" (1991a, p. 6). This approach to the everyday is also an ontological question in relation to understanding and changing.

Everyday life research is often understood as having a focus on individuals, as producing individualization. But to focus on individuals to hear their stories, their rationalities, and their wishes and dreams, does not necessarily imply individualization. The everyday is not about the *individual*—it is about the *individual-in-relations*. With the everyday starting point, it is possible to understand relations between and on different scales—an approach that threads through my research in, for instance, the concept of structural stories. Everyday practices form our understanding of the world and our way of being in the world. In Lefebvre's framing of the everyday, he argues that everyday life must be understood between the three phases of work, family and private life, and leisure. This definition underlines how people bring their whole life together when it comes to making meaning in relation to knowledge, wisdom, and power. The Danish cultural sociologist Birthe Bech-Jørgensen framed it elegantly in her book *Når hver dag bliver hverdag* (1994) (meaning "when every day becomes everyday"), where she also emphasizes that the everyday should not be divided into different spheres, but rather understood as a whole that surrounds our lives. "Everyday lives are the lives we live, maintain and renew, re-create and transform each day. Such lives cannot be defined with sociological concepts alone. What can be defined are the conditions of everyday life and the way these conditions are handled" (Bech-Jørgensen, 1994, p. 17) (my translation). Katrine Hartmann-Petersen (2020, p. 164) defines everyday life as "polyrhythmic" to emphasize the "intermingling – sometimes conflicting – multiple rhythms of urban everyday life" that individuals need to master.

Throughout history, and even today in many ways, the everyday has been underprioritized in transportation research, mostly based on the assumption that it is trivial. When I am presenting my work in transport-related settings I have often been asked if I consider policy and planning in my research. I can't remember ever hearing the same academic audience asking researchers on planning and policy if they remember to include the everyday. As such, the focus on the everyday and all its messiness, emotion, and embodied practice is placed within the largely underdeveloped sector that constitutes the institutional material arrangements for mobilities. In his *Critique of Everyday Life* (1991a), Lefebvre links this exclusion of the everyday perspective to the historical emergence of capitalism, which, as already pointed out, divided the everyday into different spheres: working, leisure, and family. Working is the productive activity, leisure takes away and distracts from being productive, and family is about propagating. The development of the capitalist society underlined the significance of productivity as that which mattered, and the trivial areas of leisure and family life related mostly to the privileged bourgeoise. In this sense, Lefebvre also indirectly argues that Marxism played a big role in rendering the everyday unimportant and trivial. With capitalism also came a renewed tension between the sciences, where a realist ontology was favored over a relativist one and the "rational economic man" became the model for understanding everyday practices. Sayer (2005) in his book *The Moral Significance of Class* calls this one of the most fundamental flaws of neoclassical economies. It is a concept that removes any need for or notion of fellow feeling and makes people all about individualistic opportunities.

The lack of attention to the everyday has changed during the last decades, not only within the mobilities paradigm but also in other sectors, not least as a result of the increased focus on climate change. It is becoming more and more difficult for a capitalist system, focused on predicting and providing on the basis of the "rational economic man," to ignore the externalities. A change in practice is needed, and this opens up a renewed interest in examining the everyday to understand the interconnectedness between the different scales of everyday life and politics and planning. Lefebvre (1991a, p. 92) already pointed this out when saying that: "Everyday life includes political life: the public consciousness, the consciousness of belonging to a society and a nation, the consciousness of class. It enters into permanent contact with the State and the State apparatus thanks to administration and bureaucracy." Today, this is an administration and bureaucracy that are increasingly trying to handle the mobile risk society and all its unintended consequences. As I already stated in the introduction, I am speaking from a Global North context. That does not, however, make this irrelevant in the Global South when many of the conditions that frame the everyday are globally distributed: the mobile risk society is not bound by national borders.

Mobile risk society

The concept of the mobile risk society originated in the theoretical work of Ulrich Beck, starting with his book *Risk Society* (1992 [1986]) which, following the Chernobyl accident in 1986, analyzes contemporary technological and ecological risks. According to Beck, these risks are an integral part of late modern lives, and they are created by science's production of (secure) knowledge. As such, the risks are "self-produced" risks, like the Chernobyl nuclear accident or the Fukushima meltdown initiated by a tsunami. In the wake of the Fukushima meltdown, Beck explained the term "self-produced" risks very precisely in a TV interview. It came from the interviewer asking Beck how to handle natural disasters so they would not have these devastating consequences. Beck started the answer by saying that there is no such thing as a natural disaster. What we have are events in nature; the disaster comes from the idea that we can control these events. Building a nuclear powerplant in an earthquake zone next to the ocean is based on a strong belief in modern technology and in the ability to control. Such risks, Beck (1997) argues, are unintended results of social activity, and they have become a driving force in modern societies. In the risk society, societal changes are often not a result of intended policies or ideologies, but are instead propelled by the need to limit the unintended consequences of modern life (Beck, 1992). Certainty is replaced with a condition of general insecurity, uncertainty, and ambivalence, forcing individuals to navigate a risky world without the social markers and clear guidance of previous times.

This does not mean that we necessarily face more risks than our ancestors, but we have a different knowledge about many more risks due to mobilities and globalization. Many of these risks are so-called second-order risks (like nuclear power or global pandemics), whose consequences travel the world and which cannot be contained or predicted (Evers and Nowotny, 1987). This produces constant risk assessment as an integral part of everyday decisions: Is it better to buy organic or locally produced vegetables? Is it safe for my kid to cycle or is it better if I drive them? How healthy is running in an urban environment because of air pollution? Which is the safest place to go on holiday in the wake of a global pandemic? The list could continue, and this bombardment of risks relies on and is also produced by expert knowledge, reflexivity, and rapid decision-making. The source of risks thereby becomes knowledge and the constant revision of knowledge, which places science in a new light in relation to its previous function as a "problem solver." In everyday life and for the individual, this means that there is no other option than to learn how to live with the multitude of risks and to develop what Beck (1997) calls "risk blindness." Especially in relation to issues such as climate change, it becomes impossible to foresee all the risks of one's own actions, and this helplessness creates risk blindness as a tool to overcome the challenge of completing everyday activities without too many ambivalences.

As a result, experts are in this sense both the authors of and the solution to self-reinforcing risk awareness. In Beck's terms, you can say it is almost impossible to separate perpetrator and victim; "You can do something, do it again, without having to be personally responsible.

One acts, so to speak, without being present" (Beck, 1997, p. 45). Here Beck is referring to the role the media plays in risk perception. Different types of media are the basis on which this reassessment of knowledge is communicated to the individual, which is why the presentation often becomes more important than the news and there is a juxtaposition of stories and topics that in reality have nothing in common other than that they have news value. This is what Giddens (1991) describes as the intrusion of distant events into everyday consciousness. These new types of media also carry with them a fundamental uncertainty about the truth of the new knowledge. The fact that different experts argue and dispute over issues is a significant source of uncertainty, especially in the knowledge that the "answer" eventually arrived at may well be revised in the future (Beck, 1992).What has become even more dominant since Beck wrote this book in 1992 is that social media has opened up a space for a whole new generation of experts, the basis for whose expertise has become increasingly blurry. With the coronavirus pandemic, this has become very evident, not least because for many social media has become the primary social contact except for close family and friends. Rulesets with different levels of severity have been put in place around the world in relation to what has been termed "social distancing" but even in places with very defined and strict rulesets there have still been many things that needed to be negotiated. This negotiation of risks has been going on in the national and international news, drawing on the knowledge of different experts, but has simultaneously been taking place on social media and also among friends and family. The corona pandemic has, apart from a long list of other things, also been marked by constant risk negotiation. Can I visit my elderly mother if we meet outside? Is it OK if I go to this meeting at work? Can I spend time with my kids even if we no longer live in the same household? Is it OK if I see my daughter today and my son tomorrow, or do I have to have five days in between? A friend of mine got COVID-19 but decided not to tell her sister and mother (with whom she had not been in physical contact) until after she was well again. The reason was that she did not have the energy to have long conversations on what she should (not) and could (not) do.

That risks are no longer something that can be contained within national borders but are developing through increased mobilities also means that cosmopolitanism is integrated in all our lives (Beck, 2018). The concept of cosmopolitanism is often misunderstood as if it describes a life on the move, traveling around the world, and the critique is that this is not true for the majority of people. In Beck's most recent book, *The Metamorphoses of the World* (2016), he explains cosmopolitanism as being closer to the everyday. Even with no access to tablets, smartphones, or travel, the price of the land our dwelling is built on and the materials used to create shelter are affected by cosmopolitan mobilities. There is (almost) no way to avoid cosmopolitanism when it infuses, at the very least, all the institutional material arrangements framing the everyday. The world is centered around mobilities with all the (perceived) risk this entails. The close interconnectedness between mobilities and the perception of diverse risk which strongly influences the lives of people all over the globe led Kesselring (2008a) to develop the concept of a "mobile risk society." This key concept synthesizes theories of reflexive modernization and the risk society (Beck, 1992; Beck et al., 2003) with the mobilities paradigm (Sheller and Urry, 2016) and helps us understand mobilization and globalization as risk-inducing general principles of modern life: "...the rise of mobilities on every scale of society—from the body to the global— radicalizes the risk society and shows the global interconnectedness and the inescapable character of the social and spatial mobilization of modernity" (Kesselring, 2008a, p. 92). As an example to illustrate these structural changes, Kesselring refers to a previous study on highways (or "motorways" as he calls them). In the 1970s and 1980s, a highway had a destination at each end, like the highway from Nuremberg to Munich or Paris to Lyon, and it had a name that was related to those place-names. Today these same highways are called the E9 or E7, part of the Trans-European Network (TEN) and, as Kesselring says, today "Motorways are scapes of flow, not identification" (Kesselring, 2008a, p. 92). On the everyday scale, the mobile risk society helps us understand the ambivalences of the risk-inducing and carbon-reliant systems of mobilities integrated in contemporary everyday life. This "second modernity" is a time where the materials and cultures of systems of mobilities are essential for all our everyday activities.

Already in 1986, when Beck wrote *Risk Society*, he argued that extensive risks would transform society and create a "second modernity." The first modernity, as Beck describes it, is marked by stability, unambiguity, ideology, class distinctions, and traditions providing lives with direction, orientation, and predictability. In the second modernity, risk, ambivalence, insecurity, and reflexivity are prominent, influencing lives with non-directionality and permanent and active boundary management (Beck, 1992). Kesselring (2008a, 2019) moves the discussion even further and suggest a possible third modernity where individuals are mobile hybrids, where automation and digitalization provide a presumed order and security.

The modes for movement are very significant for how society develops in the mobile risk society. In the first modernity, the train is the mode that can move masses, providing stable connections, clear structures, and timetables. The train was perceived as the "one-best-way" solution for fast, direct, and reliable movement of goods and people and embodied qualities such as stability, unambiguity, and heteronomy. In the second modernity, the collective solutions are increasingly replaced with the private car, a technology socially and culturally structured around individualization, autonomy, and fluidity. The third modernity is based on "motile hybrids" that are as yet unknown constellations of bodies and technologies where physical spaces, knowledge, and skills are in constant flow. The melding of humans, digital tools, and technologies is a modernism characterized by pluralism, networks, and fragmented mobilities where ambivalence is normality, and temporality dominates policy and planning (Kesselring, 2008a, 2019). Current social and political developments suggest that part of what Kesselring is speculating about has already come true. We are not yet hybrids, but on the other hand consider mechanical hearts and titanium hips. Sociologist Anthony Elliot talks about *Reinvention* (2021, p. 9 [2013]), describing a constant professional and personal striving "...including Botox and makeover mantras as well as endless corporate downsizing.... " In his book *Identity Troubles* (2016), Elliot describes a shift where plasticity, flexibility, and adaptability become essential characteristics of what we might call a third modernity. He underlines how identity is bound up with mobilities and movement, and to this I would add the social practices and perceptions deeply rooted in the everyday in a mobile risk society. Zooming in on this everyday life and trying to understand what living in a mobile risk society actually means for perceptions of and changes in mobilities and their systems means establishing a lens for exploring how practices, relations, and exclusion processes and ideas form specific cultures of mobilities. In a time where volatility and flexibility are at center stage and no "one-best-way" or optimal solutions are available, we need to create rationalities to guide the organization of everyday life.

How to give voice to that we come to take for granted

Very often, the further away you are from things the clearer they appear. Twenty years ago, when I was a student, I became interested in everyday life and transport. Today I know it was not transport, it was mobilities, but at that time, the term did not yet exist in the vocabulary. I was studying in a problem-based, transdisciplinary education system with a focus on technological, environmental, and social science and a major emphasis on environmental planning. At this time, in the 1990s, Denmark had a traffic and environment fund managed by the Ministry of Environment. Municipalities could apply for money to make improvements to the environment and traffic safety. Many roundabouts, some bike paths, and some bus lanes were constructed using this money.

A small amount of the money was used for projects aimed at changing everyday transport practices—moving people from cars to buses and bikes. In the projects, people were given things like bikes, cycle trailers, and bus tickets and the projects managed to change people's practices—but only for a short while. Within one year, most participants were back to their old habits (using the car for all trips). Trying to understand why this happened was the subject of one of my first student projects. From the beginning, the approach was qualitative interviews and focus groups—to collect detailed descriptions of the reasons why everyday mobilities practice was so routinized and the significance of this. With a transdisciplinary education, transport was not only viewed through models but also discussed in relation to the Multi-Level Perspective (MLP) and the Social Construction of Technology (SCOT). In many ways, these theoretical concepts explained the politics, meanings, and ideas embedded in a technology very well, but their perspective on everyday practice was very limited. The emotional, philosophical, and embodied elements of everyday practices, which were apparent in my interviews, had no place in these theories. My work with the concept of structural stories came out of a need to find a place for the emotional and ethical aspects of late modern lives. When John Urry's book *Mobilities* came out in 2007, this was very precisely described: "There is too much transport in the study of travel and not enough society and thinking through the complex intersecting relations between society and transport" (Urry, 2007, p. 20). The need to understand the complex intersections in movement, to disrupt path-dependent ways of movement and change to more sustainable mobilities, was the driver behind the creation of structural stories.

The development of structural stories

The concept of structural stories was developed in projects focusing on everyday practice in relation to the car and public transportation (Freudendal-Pedersen, 2009, 2015a, 2020). The structural story illustrates the rationalities we create, the stories we construct to explain our practices and that are formulated as universal truths, like: "When one has kids one needs a car." Some structural stories are context specific, while others, like the one about kids and cars, are relatively universal. The dominance of the car in policy and planning is created by structural stories supported in everyday life and that feed back into policy and planning. Another structural story about cars, "one gets more freedom when one has a car," is also heard very often, in politics and in car commercials to give two examples. Although there is plenty of research that shows the unfreedom the car also produces, both for those inside and those outside the car, this does not disrupt the use of this structural story. As a former transport minister in Denmark said not that many years ago, "We become freer and richer with the car." That the car equals freedom plays an important role on the high value society places on cars and thus facilitates public acceptance of the need for the associated infrastructure (Freudendal-Pedersen, 2009; Notar, 2012; Sheller, 2004; Urry, 2007).

The concept of structural stories arose after an interview with a couple in their 50s who had recently become "empty nesters." When I asked why they had a car, the reply was "When one has kids one needs a car." By asking this very direct question at the end of a long conversation, they replied by evoking the quick response that in most situations would generate a nod and an "of course" as a response. Everybody agrees on this. The generalized "one" and the "of course" response is what makes it a structural story. That it becomes a structural story does not mean that it is not true, it can be very true in many specific situations; the problem is that it becomes a generalized truth that produces and reproduces specific practices. When researching car usage, it was clear that when people were pregnant or planning to be pregnant, this was a frequently used story. Buying a car was in line with buying a changing table, a baby carriage, and so forth. In this way, the structural stories as representing something taken for granted create a relationship between kids and cars—you need to buy a pram, a changing table, diapers… and a car. The structural story is not based on measurable and material circumstances. Rather, it is about creating rationalities that simplify choices and are confirmed by individuals-in-relations. In this sense, the structural story is *equally* true for everybody who uses it, because it helps to navigate *their* everyday lives. Even if, with measurements of distance and time, we see a difference between two households and the need for the car, it does not necessarily relate to their experience of everyday life and will not affect their practice. With the structural stories, the aim is not to understand individuals per se, but rather individuals-in-relations producing and reproducing specific rationalities about mobilities practice.

The need for structural stories in a mobile risk society

The mobile risk society is framing everyday practices, and the structural stories emerge due to the constant demands for choices to be made and risks to be assessed, thus creating ambivalence (Bauman, 2000; Beck, 1992, 1997; Giddens, 1991). The aim is to have everyday life components, that together make it possible to achieve "the good life." The components are influenced by societal discourses on what makes a good parent, how to be an adaptable and flexible worker, and how to live healthily, and the glue that makes it all work is mobilities (Bissell, 2019; Freudendal-Pedersen, 2009; Pooley et al., 2006; Thomsen, 2005). When the everyday is organized, it is not the issue of mobilities that is discussed or negotiated, it is the different components. If anybody questions the aspects of the choices that are taken for granted, the structural story comes into play. In this way, the structural stories reinforce the advantages of specific modes of mobilities as indisputable "objective truths," and changing practice is out of the question. The structural elements in the stories are inspired by Giddens' (1984) concept of structuration, where actors and structures are not viewed as two independent dimensions. Society is not viewed as either just the experience of the actor or an existing social structure, but rather practice spread over time and space (Giddens, 1984, p. 2). Society is a constant process of structuration where practice is simultaneously both structuring and being structured by society. The structures are embedded in people's consciousness and reproduced when acting, while already-existing structures are influencing their actions. Through everyday mobilities practice, the structural stories are produced and reproduced and thereby contribute to the need for specific mobilities. The structural story can be seen as a micro-discourse that illustrates hegemonies in everyday practices, hegemonies that are reified and institutionalized. It illuminates practices taken for granted and how individuals-in-relations tell stories that create resonance and thereby maintain specific practices.

The structural story also relates to Berger and Luckmann's (1966) concept of reification, "the apprehension of the products of human activity *as if* they were something other than human products" (1966, p. 106). I once had an interviewee tell me that we had as little influence on how much car transport there is as the potatoes had when they became widespread in Europe. This is a perfect example of reification where everyday practices are defined outside of individual control, and become something that is imposed upon us. The system of auto-mobilities is reified on all scales of society, and the structural story is what is used when ambivalence arises. That the car is the only oppor-tunity becomes an objective fact, with no possibility of or control over changing it. With the structural story, we can see how everyday prac-tices create reified and institutionalized discourses. Other structural stories, for instance "one cannot let the kids cycle to school, it is too dangerous, it is safer to drive them," are part of institutionalizing the car's dominance. Structural stories have, in one way or another, been part of my research since I developed them and when you start paying attention, they are everywhere.

Another structural story that supports high levels of car ownership is "one cannot rely on public transport; it is always delayed," and this is one I often hear in the media. My favorite example is from one of the big Danish news media that were reporting on the reconstruction of a road running above a busy train station. That the road needed reconstruction meant that they had to place scaffolding down on the train tracks. The trains could still run on the track but, of course, had to reduce their speed. An additional problem was that the scaffold-ing was placed at the entrance to a 3-km tunnel through which all of Copenhagen's trains have to pass. The road maintenance created a lot of delays in train traffic. To mollify the delayed passengers, the Danish State Railways offered them coffee and candy. The presentation on the news was that typically trains were always delayed and that the Danish State Railways thought that they could sweeten the situation by doing this. At no point was it mentioned that it was the need for road renovations that had caused the delays for train passengers. This is just one of many examples of how structural stories also appear in the media and are being reproduced. I currently spend a lot of time looking into how structural stories can be challenged by new stories and in many ways this is also driving this book. When in Chapters 45 I discuss communities, emotions, and utopias, it is driven by the search for new stories about what makes the good life with sustainable mobilities possible.

At the beginning of this chapter I framed the everyday as an episte-mological starting point and the function and institutionalization of structural stories is a very good example thereof. The question "What is the scale of the research?" can be useful, and is important, but can also be very limiting. With structuration and reification, it is clear that social processes and discourses travel between many scales. When I say I do research on an everyday scale, it is true, but also not really enough. I do research on an everyday scale to understand why things matter to people so I can better understand a policy and planning scale. At the same time, inspired by Sayers' (2005, 2011) discussions on normativity, the focus on the everyday helps in understanding aspects of policy and planning. Focusing on understanding the everyday scale of everyday mobilities is a starting point for research on how to change the dominant unsustainable mobilities systems. The significance of the banal and the trivial is highly underestimated, and creating sustainable futures without taking this seriously is an impossible task. If we want to change practices, we need to take practice seriously.

Methodologies to search for everyday rationalities

The exploration of practices, the creation of meaning and understanding of everyday life dreams and hopes, requires qualitative methodologies. A reflexive methodology that is flexible and able to follow the research on unexpected paths and that welcomes normativity as inevitable opens up the analysis (Alvesson and Sköldberg, 2000; Freudendal-Pedersen et al., 2010). The research that I build upon in this book is based on a qualitative reflexive methodology. Through in-depth qualitative interviews, everyday practices, focused on mobilities but also related to whatever other issues arise in the conversations, have been investigated (Freudendal-Pedersen et al., 2010; Kvale, 1996). Using a controlled variation between abstract and concrete questions, many interesting and philosophical conversations about seemingly abstract questions regarding freedom, community, and emotions have taken place.

For some researchers, asking questions like "what is freedom to you?" might seem too abstract. In my experience, this can be quite a productive line of questioning, falling between questions like "describe a typical everyday life" and "tell me when you moved here and why." Even if the respondents are not ready to give a clear answer to an abstract question at the outset, the issue usually appears later in the conversation. The greatest degree of resistance to this type of question I remember was from a 50-year-old businessman. When I asked him the abstract freedom question, he protested and said, "I didn't think we were going to talk about this kind of stuff." I accepted this rejection, and we spent the next 20 minutes with him explaining to me everything about his new technological mobility gadget. However, interestingly, later in the interview he embarked on long philosophical reflections on freedom, what it means, how freedom is not something everybody has access to, and how significant the feeling of freedom, especially related to mobility, was to him. This is a very illustrative example of what might be labeled the rational economic man, but, in this interview, he showed all the emotional rationalities also existed, even if we are not used to talking about them.

Focus groups were organized after the interviews, especially so in the case of projects that were concentrating on the structural stories. This gave insight into the negotiation and construction of meaning and significance (Halkier, 2010). In the focus groups, participants validated rationalities and the use value of structural stories in larger forums became visible. One method that stimulated many structural stories was providing pictures of different transport modes and asking participants to order the pictures based on different elements like "what creates the most freedom," "what is best for the environment," and so forth. To push the discussion a little further, they are asked to agree on the result. This creates a different form of argumentation, involving the exchanging of points of view but which is more about using the right arguments to convince people. If the situation or the tone becomes anywhere close to unpleasant, they are told they do not need to agree and that disagreements are also interesting. By progressing the discussion in this way, the negotiations and the use of structural stories come to the foreground. In the focus groups, it is significant that many more structural stories are used when the people in the group do not know each other. Another method is presenting participants with quotes from the individual interviews (with permission from the interviewees, of course). This method gives a good insight into how they "defend" their own practices and how others carefully criticize or support, very often with the use of a structural story. With a structural story, the criticism is not aimed at the person who gave the quote, but is "a general statement about the world that everybody agrees on." Finally, when the focus group is drawing to a close, I present the concepts I am researching and ask them to discuss these or reflect on them. This has provided many interesting reflections that have broadened my views and driven the analysis in new directions.

Ethnographic research carried out by various organizations operating, directly or indirectly, in the field of mobilities and in both urban and non-urban areas provides knowledge on the institutional material arrangements, thereby creating a different starting point for interviews. Using a GoPro camera when moving around can give a different awareness of the rhythms and help discover new facets of mobilities. The awareness of how you turn your head, the small movements you make to avoid danger, becomes more intense when you use the GoPro. Also, it provides material that I have used on several occasions when

I have been presenting abroad to, for instance, *show* what cycling in Copenhagen is.

The last methodology I will mention here is workshops inspired by the action research future-creating workshop (Aagaard Nielsen and Svensson, 2006; Jungk and Müllert, 1987). These kinds of workshops have a variety of aims. First, they can be used to create a common direction (utopia) as a starting point for working on a specific long-term project or as a method to create future utopias as part of shorter projects. Second, the workshops create a community with whom experiences can be shared and lessons learned. The communities the workshops create can help support the results of the workshop if and when they are put into practice. These workshops always have a specific question to guide them, are run according to a specific set of rules for communication, and use a variety of creative, sensual, playful, and imaginative tools for generating ideas. The workshops take a traditional approach divided into three phases: a critique phase, a phase of visions, and a realization phase. In one project I, together with Sven Kesselring, developed two additional phases: a phase zero focusing on creating a common ground from which to start the work and a phase four focusing on visualizing the results.

The empirical work has been with groups of diverse ages and education levels. As is very common, especially in Copenhagen where the majority of my interviewees are from, they use a variety of transport modes and cannot be labeled solely as car drivers, public transport users, or cyclists. In terms of socioeconomic status, my interviewees primarily belong to the middle-class, which is relatively large in Denmark due to its welfare society (Freudendal-Pedersen 2014a). This large middle-class possesses significant power through their jobs and through the impact of their voices when it comes to validating and recreating stories.

Understanding the making of meaning in practice

In this book, interview quotes are used without any details on background and context. This choice is based on the aim of focusing on the making of meaning. I am not suggesting that, for instance, gender and age are not relevant to understanding aspects of everyday practices, but preconceptions about their significance can blur the understanding. This is also related to transportation research, where the focus is on behavior instead of practice. It is an ontology where rational factors such as time, money, and location dominate and changing behavior is about providing knowledge so people decide to change—it is a cognitive matter (Mattauch et al., 2016). The approaches most often used to unlock this behavior are related to sociological concepts such as ideal types, lifestyle categories, and living patterns. The ideal type (Weber, 1949) comes out of a synthesis of individual phenomena. The "pure" type cannot be found in "reality" but is a combination of individuals and functions as a way of creating order in a complex reality. They are often used to categorize "the passionate driver" or "the devoted public transport user" and serves as a guideline on how to make this ideal type change. Living patterns, with Hägerstraand's (1970) time-geography as cornerstone, focus on time and space as that which tells us something about how large socioeconomic environmental mechanisms work. Here the location becomes essential for the choices of individuals ("when you live on the countryside you need a car"). Most socioeconomic models used within transport and urban planning are related to this correlation. Lifestyle, originally Max Weber's *Lebensstile*, was developed by Pierre Bourdieu, in particular to explain social structures and inequalities as that which forms everyday practices. With Anthony Giddens (1991), the concept is also used to explain how a lifestyle entails habits and orientations that provide ontological security, by not having to reflect on whether or not to use a car. With my focus on structural stories and storytelling, I have found elements of all three of the above categorizations in my empirical material. The interviewees vary in terms of age, gender, socioeconomic status, and geographies, but they all have the same kind of structural stories as part of their explanations for their choice of mobilities in everyday life.

My interest has been to investigate how interviewees "rationalize" *their* everyday practice and focus on the stories. Preconceptions about matters such as gender, place of residence, and education are often what we use as navigation tools to understand practice, and these types of explanations can blur the ability to hear the common stories. These stories that underline how everyday life is practiced must be studied in relation to its links with all levels and scales of society, not as an isolated and unrelated item. Birte Bech-Jørgensen (1994) defined everyday life as the lives we live, maintain and renew, re-create and transform each day, and such lives cannot themselves be defined. What can be defined is the conditions under which these lives are lived and how these conditions are handled. In this understanding, it is the interconnectedness that is central. Amin and Thrift (2002) touched upon this in their book *Cities: Reimagining the Urban*, where they say that it seems understanding cities stops at the doorstep to people's homes. This barrier between the home and the city needs to be removed because stories travel and in doing so they construct everyday life and society through the mobilities of people, things, and ideas (Urry, 2000, 2007).

This also helps to clarify the fact that those structural stories should not be explained by individualizing them; instead the focus needs to be on how they are reified and institutionalized when individuals-in-relations tell stories that create resonance and thereby maintain specific practices. This will be the starting point throughout this book. The empirical material comes from the following research projects: *Inbetween Freedom and Unfreedom* (2003–2007), funded by the Danish State Railways and Roskilde University and focusing on the comprehension of everyday life mobilities and how this affects mobility practice (Freudendal-Pedersen, 2005, 2007, 2009, 2015a); *Urban Cycle Mobilities* (2012–2015), funded by the Danish Council for Independent Research and focusing on why people cycle (Freudendal-Pedersen, 2014a, 2015a, 2015b, 2018, 2021); *Mobilities Futures and the City* (2014–2016), funded by Aalborg University and Roskilde University in Denmark, an interdisciplinary experimental project to develop powerful "stories" on the good mobile life in cities (Freudendal-Pedersen and Kesselring, 2016; Kesselring and Freudendal-Pedersen, 2021); and *Sustainable Innovative Mobility Solutions* (2019–2023), funded by Innovation Fund Denmark and focusing on sustainable mobility solutions tailored to the everyday life of citizens in three Copenhagen neighborhoods (two central, one suburban) (Freudendal-Pedersen et al., 2020). Interview quotes from these four projects will be used in Chapter 4 to unfold the significance and the simultaneous fluidity of communities on the move, as well as to elaborate on the significance of emotions when planning for future sustainable mobilities in Chapter 5. Before getting to this, the following chapter outlines some of the institutional material arrangements that frame everyday life mobilities.

3 Planning for technology or people—the human scale

In Chapter 2, the focus was on everyday life and its mobilities in the mobile risk society. In this chapter, the focus is on understanding how the institutional material arrangements of mobilities have been developed, how they define what is possible in the current situation, and what this means for creating a pathway toward future sustainable mobilities. Our urban landscapes have been highly influenced by a rational planning paradigm developed during the first modernity that aimed to create healthy places for people in the aftermath of World War II. It was a time characterized by unambiguity, ideology, and traditions that provided direction, orientation, and predictability (Galland and Tewdwr-Jones, 2019). In relation to mobilities, this meant great hope and trust in technology and its ability to change the world for the better. With the risk, ambivalence, insecurity, and reflexivity characterizing the second modernity, a focus on the unintended consequences stemming from the planning decisions of the first modernity emerged. This also entailed questioning the focus on technology as the starting point for creating better mobilities and better lives. Even with the huge amount of knowledge on the unintended consequences arising from our current mobilities systems, the form and function of movement in cities are still to a very high degree marked by a tradition of "predict and provide." This is based on the belief that efficient transportation is the gateway to a wealthier society, and this most often means transportation with the private car. This also means sticking to the predict-and-provide system approach because it ensures the stability of the current economic system. This, of course, would not be the case if we were to radically change the socioeconomic transport models to include many more of the unintended consequences of our current transportation system, but attempts to do this have so far been unsuccessful (Næss et al., 2014). I recently supervised a student whose master's thesis dealt with parking politics

DOI: 10.4324/9781003100515-3

in a new (sustainable) development area in Copenhagen. In the project, she carried out qualitative interviews with different stakeholders in the planning and development of this urban area. One of the very interesting results from her report came from stakeholders responsible for the final development (development companies, entrepreneurs, etc.). They were very clear that they were not interested in building for how mobilities would be in ten years, they only wanted to focus on the current situation. When the current situation in Copenhagen is increasing car ownership, this means more parking spaces.

Transport planning is indeed significant for the creation, maintenance, and functioning of urban agglomerations, but the issue is more which kind of transport we are planning for. Within the mobilities research tradition, the focus is on understanding the significance of mobilities for societies, economies, and the social in a globalized world. This means also taking into account how the social develops with mobilities: to see the opportunities as well as the inequalities. It is not enough to predict what the future might look like based on how things currently function and are distributed. For instance, in the city of Copenhagen 30% of the CO_2 emissions come from road traffic, of which 70% is attributed to private cars (City of Copenhagen, 2019). The Copenhagen numbers fit the EU average and underline how the technology of the private car is firmly embedded in everyday life. Nigel Thrift (2004, p. 41) points this out when saying that: "…a hundred years or so after the birth of automobility, the experience of driving is sinking in to our 'technological unconscious' and producing a phenomenology that we increasingly take for granted." However, while it may currently be taken for granted, the costs involved in planning for ever-increasing numbers of cars in the future strongly suggest we need to change this approach.

For changes to be made—as with the focus on everyday life practices—it is necessary to focus also on the materialities and the unintended consequences of current systems. In this chapter, I will address the institutional material arrangements and the concepts used when providing the movements and systems dominating the urban. The meaning and significance of these concepts varies depending on the institution or person using them, while some have developed over time to assume broader or different meanings. These concepts therefore arise as a result of the historical context of their creation and development, and also as a result of the evolution of new research areas. Here I provide a short overview of some of the concepts in transport and mobilities research that form the field. The intention is not to provide an in-depth understanding of all the various research fields working with these concepts in numerous ways, but knowing about these different research approaches is a prerequisite for understanding the materialities that constitute the starting point for our current transportation system and also for changing these systems of movement that dominate the world today. Working across these different concepts also involves engaging in dialogue with different scientific traditions. In other words, to understand the current system and be able to steer it in a more sustainable direction requires a basic comprehension of the institutional material arrangements supporting it.

Mobilities and cities as interconnected

The Industrial Revolution produced a number of inventions that fundamentally changed the conditions for transport. From only being able to transport goods and people over relatively short distances using human or animal power, the invention of the steam engine, and thus rail transport, made it possible for land transport to cover long distances in a short time. Both speed and capacity increased rapidly and lead to increased industrial specialization as a result of manufacturing being located independent of natural resources. Food production moved out of the cities and those cities grew accordingly, facilitated by new transportation systems (Hanson, 1995; Steel, 2008). Other important developments in the nineteenth century were the development of the steam ship, which increased the speed of global transport, and telegraphy, which meant that communication became instant and independent of transport.

The history of traffic and transportation modes illuminates how they changed lives, economies, urban form, and many other aspects of the world (Tarr, 1989; Urry, 2007; Wolf, 1996). Of special significance for our modern world was the development of the combustion engine, and thus the automobile, in the late nineteenth century, followed by the construction of the highways they required. The first successful manned powered flight took off in 1903 and, following World War I, airplanes were increasingly used to transport people and goods over long distances. In the 1950s, the introduction of containers meant massive efficiency gains in freight transport, facilitating and accelerating globalization. In the 1960s, international air travel became easily accessible and along with the growth in automobiles and motorways led to a decline in the demand for rail transport. This development made it possible to spread activities (shopping, working, education, leisure) over larger distances and cities needed to be planned in a way that would facilitate the car.

Le Corbusier (1947) is often seen as the front runner in this development. Le Corbusier had a utopian vision of creating green, clean, and safe environments for people to dwell in, but what is most remembered today is how he imagined this through segregation of traffic. What remains as a legacy is his contribution to the International Congress of Modern Architecture (1928–1959) (CIAM) planning doctrine that achieved a major significance in planning urban transportation. In Chapter 5, I will address the utopian and visionary aspects of Le Corbusier's work, but here the focus is on the legacy of his ideas regarding the possible benefits the urban form could gain from efficient transportation. CIAM was formed by 28 European architects seeking to formalize architectural principles of modernity. From the outset, they worked on the basis that architecture should be used as a political and economic tool and created a planning doctrine for a functional city where social issues could be resolved through strict functional segregation.

> Zoning that takes account of the key functions—housing, work, recreation—will bring order in the urban territory. Traffic, the fourth function, must have only one aim: to bring the other three usefully into communication (Debord and Wolman 1956 in Sadler, 1999, p. 24).

This was a time when the car was entering the everyday life and the opportunities and fascination associated with this technology were all-pervasive. It was a time when many people moved out into the suburbs, seeking the fresh air and additional space the dirty and polluted city centers lacked. For those who did not dream of or could not afford their own house, Le Corbusier's conception of "the Radiant City," composed of skyscrapers within a park, became the vision for many modern housing areas. Le Corbusier wanted to integrate the car into the city, and "separation" and "flow" were key words. The concept was large arterial roads for cars without crossroads to keep pedestrian in their own pathways developed alongside these roads (cyclists were not really considered at this time). The intention was that car traffic should not be interrupted and efficiency and wide spaces to facilitate the avoidance of public interaction were the outline:

> Our fast car takes the special elevated motor track between the majestic skyscrapers: as we approach nearer, there is seen the repetition against the sky of the twenty-four skyscrapers; to our left and right on the outskirts of every particular area are the

municipal and administrative buildings; and enclosing the space are the museums and university buildings. The whole city is a park (Le Corbusier, in Jacobs, 1961, p. 21).

With the Radiant City, Le Corbusier presented an orderly and clear vision of a city which for many years was the prime goal for city planners and architects. Till Koglin (2013) shows through a comparison between cycling in Stockholm and Copenhagen how the idea of separation resulted in the prioritization of motorized traffic. The current argument used for this prioritization is traffic safety and traffic flow, but the idea is basically the same. In his work, Koglin illustrates this with pictures, created in accordance with the Swedish SCAFT principles (Principles for Urban Planning with Respect to Road Safety). The illustrations provided to planners have a "right" and "wrong" headline, making it clear what "good" transport planning is.

With these planning systems, the private car and logistic networks became the central focus of city planning (Dennis and Urry, 2009; Newman and Kenworthy, 2015), and today the unintended consequences of these planning strategies are the main item on the planning agenda for many cities around the world. The Urban Age program at the London School of Economics has gathered knowledge on cities around the world and discussed (among other things) the implications of prevailing planning strategies. In one of their publications, *The Endless City*, Sudjic (2007, p. 35) sums up as follows: "...it may well be that cities are more often the product of unintended consequences than of anything else." The work they did with planners around the world showed how in many cities the prioritization of the car and of buildings designed to accommodate its free flow had killed city life due to a firm belief that flow and effectiveness was the way to economic prosperity. With this vision, public life on the street became a thing of the past and had to be erased so that the streets could become places of flow for motorized traffic, symbolizing modernity itself.

Traffic

Aiming to provide the basic facilities and services so that a given activity can take place or for a given function in a community to be available, the construction of infrastructure has been a major project during the twentieth century. In the case of infrastructure in this context, the service or activity would most commonly be movement of people or objects. These "systems of traffic" consist of roads or other pathways for movement, terminals for conducting and organizing movements, traffic-steering systems, service and supply networks, and most importantly, modes of transport adjusted to these systems. In the case of road transportation, these could be cars, trucks, buses, bikes, pedestrians, or whichever modes of transport that can adjust to the landscape provided by roads. Traffic represents a quantifiable figure of these modes of transport. How many cars, trucks, bikes, pedestrians, buses, or skateboarders use a given street crossing within a given timeframe, or are taking a given trip for a given purpose? These examples show in a simple manner how traffic is measured and thus conceptually captured.

Infrastructure consists of structures that point beyond themselves. The sufficient conditions to fulfill the purpose of their construction are not present until the infrastructure is actually used. The purpose, functions, effects, or implications of infrastructure are understood through the notion of traffic. Utilizing the word "traffic" as a representation of the circulation of people, objects, and services, the structures are given a purpose and an organizing task of providing and reproducing desirable conditions for traffic. For most infrastructure, it is evident that economic advantages exist as a result of more people using it, which is also of significance for interconnectedness. Benefiting from the extension of infrastructure can be seen as a politically regulated objective, thus often placing governmental creation and regulation of infrastructure as the central organizing force. Regimes of public government carry out the role of planning, building, and maintaining physical infrastructure, while the users are both civil society and private companies. Traffic is reproduced as a result of the need for connectivity and can be depicted as a function of time, as movements between spatial relations, or the knitting together of economic activities. The different representations of traffic may thus be understood through the rhythms of a city according to working hours or school schedules, through the geographical patterns of residential areas and their relative proximity to opportunities for work, shopping, or leisure activities, or in terms of economic activity and trade relations between cities, regions, or within and between different systems of production (see for instance Cheng and Chen, 2015; Krasheninnikov, 2019; Kurth et al., 2020).

Entering into the realms of traffic related to information and images, more dimensions need to be added. Handling the different intensities and densities of traffic has implications that are not only physical, they also relate to how movement within the infrastructure is organized and regulated. The accommodation of traffic is thus infrastructure, the systems operating within infrastructure as well as what constitutes the rules within these structures. The different modes of traffic can only function with specific systems of regulations providing technical installation systems, classified by type, e.g., heavy motor vehicles (car, truck), other vehicles (motorbike, bicycle), and pedestrians. These systems regulate the options and possibilities for movement, mainly through technical installations such as traffic lights, Intelligent Transportation Systems (ITS), congestion charge schemes, traffic cameras, logistics management systems, and ticketing machines. These technical installations represent certain ways of regulating traffic that interact directly with its flow to achieve and sustain certain ways of organizing it. This is one way of understanding the materialization of an organizing system around transportation, but the formal rules of traffic systems are also integrated as signs or norms. The rules ordering traffic can be, for instance, marked lanes, junctions, intersections, interchanges, traffic signals, or traffic signs. Some jurisdictions may have very detailed and complex rules of the road using physical representations, while others rely more on drivers' common sense and willingness to cooperate and can be seen as the informal rules developed over time, facilitating the flow of traffic through interactions between the individual users (see for instance Chen et al., 2017; Lan and Cai, 2021; Munford, 2017; Rahimi and Hakimpour, 2018).

Traffic is border crossing. One rule that applies to most modern cities is traffic signals whose colors and intentions can be read globally. When there are no signs or markings, different rules are observed depending on the location. At international level, the Vienna Convention on Road Signs and Signals, prescribing standardized traffic control devices (signs, signals, and markings), represents an attempt to standardize traffic rules. The reason why traffic is regulated is in order to produce a better combination of travel safety and efficient use of the infrastructure's capacity. This is where the term "accessibility" as an important concept in traffic regulations comes into play. In terms of traffic management, accessibility is most threatened by jams and gridlocks, and traffic regulation seeks to avoid this by simulating organized traffic and applying queuing theory, stochastic processes, and equations of mathematical physics to its flows.

With the building of these systems traffic has increased, and today (ITS are used to distribute traffic and create more accessibility, e.g., avoiding congestion. An ITS is a system of hardware, software, and operators that allow better monitoring and control of traffic in order to optimize traffic flow. It is based around a number of technologies that monitor traffic flows through the use of sensors, live cameras, or by analyzing data from cellular phones in cars and then rerouting traffic by providing information about alternative routes and travel times.

Systems of infrastructure facilitating traffic are very much part of political negotiations, both within a country but also very much in relation to global networks. Infrastructure has a long lifespan, and thus these decisions have binding long-term consequences in relation to the development of cities, nations, and the world. As a publication from the Ministry of Traffic in Denmark says about a hundred years of traffic development, "Regulating traffic is done in a context of eternity" (Trafikministeriet, 2000, p. 9) [own translation]. With these infrastructural traffic systems and the traffic that accompanies them, the movements of people and goods must be properly understood in order to optimize the system. This is where transport research steps in.

Transport

Transport is the direct empirical representation of the movement of people and goods from one location to another. It is traceable, quantifiable, and something we can see with our own eyes. It is performed by various modes, such as air, rail, road, and water. The function of transportation is seen as increasing the relative value of people or objects by moving them from where they are to another, preferred destination. Transportation research clarifies and elucidates these activities by analyzing patterns of movement and calculating the economic costs and the spatial and environmental impacts of transportation activities, using socioeconomic models for making planning decisions. Engineers and planners have traditionally been the main scientific traditions working within transportation research and the central goal has been to remove impediments to transport, thereby facilitating the process for an increased number of people. Research has traditionally been centered on questions of accessibility, risk, infrastructure optimization, the impact of noise, and other environmental considerations (see for instance Sharifi et al., 2021; Walker et al., 2011; Wang et al., 2020).

Throughout history, transport has been a spur to expansion and has been seen as a key necessity for specialization—allowing the production and consumption of products or services to occur at different locations. Transport allows more trade over larger distances and a greater spread of people and labor. Thus economic growth has always been interlinked with increasing transport capacity and rationality. Transport is a key component of modern society, enabling and dictating a physical distinction between home and work, forcing people to transport themselves to places of work or study, as well as to temporarily relocate for other daily activities. Transport is essential for many firms today, not only in relation to logistics but also because commerce requires the movement of people to conduct business. This transporting of people can be either to allow face-to-face communication for important decisions or to move specialists from their regular place of work to sites where they are needed. It is also the essence of most leisure activities, including tourism.

The transport of people and the transport of goods (logistics) are two different research areas with different traditions. This is not necessarily the case within traffic regulation where the systems, e.g., terminals such as airports, ports, and stations, the locations where passengers and freight can be transferred from one vehicle or mode to another, can be part of the same infrastructural system. Still, there is a big difference between passenger and logistic intermodality. For passenger transport, intermodality is about integrating different modes to allow travelers to change between different modes in order to reach a specific destination quickly and with a minimum of friction. This can be stations interconnecting buses, trains, and metros, or airport rail links connecting airports to the city centers and suburbs. Cars and bikes are today implemented in intermodal systems to a higher degree than was previously the case; this can be in the form of biking racks and parking facilities, but also as city bike systems and shared cars (see for instance Fernández et al., 2021; Goletz et al., 2020; Weliwitiya et al., 2019).

In relation to freight, transport terminals act as transshipment points, and freight transport, or shipping, is a key factor in the manufacturing value chain. With increased specialization and globalization, production is often located far away from consumption and freight can travel long distances, being repacked on the way to the consumer, thus increasing the demand for transport. Logistics refers to the entire process of transferring products from producer to consumer, including storage, transport, transshipment, warehousing, handling of materials, and packaging, with associated exchanges of information. However, some cargo is transported directly from the point of production to the point of use.

Transport planning and transport research focus on allowing high utilization and less impact in relation to new infrastructure. The main tool in transport planning is transport models; these are used to forecast future transport patterns and function as the backbone of regulation policy creation by authorities. The technical universities are the traditional choice for training transport planners, educating traffic engineers, planning for municipalities, states, and so forth. Transport engineering is a subdiscipline of civil engineering, dedicated to issues such as trip generation, trip distribution, mode choice, and route assignment, while the operative level is handled through traffic engineering. Transport is more and more becoming a transdisciplinary research field, still dominated by engineers and economists, but psychologists, sociologists, political scientists, geographers, and anthropologists have increasingly been adding new angles.

The overall idea of transport as an individual's rational choice when getting from A to B is prevalent within transport research. The choices of individuals within transport research are primarily investigated through notions of comfort, time, or economy (Geurs and van Wee, 2004). The insight into transport-choice patterns, understood as rational individual valuation of available alternatives, gives a basis for calculating the consequences of changes within the transport systems. Transportation is not traditionally seen as an act that contains value in itself (Cole, 2005), but rather as an intermediary between a place or state of relatively low value and one with a relatively higher one. Putting objects or people in motion has a natural purpose of getting them to a destination in the fastest and least expensive way possible. The investigation of these patterns results in models, calculations, and analyses of spatial transformations, providing or uncovering evidence to show the effectiveness of specific modes of transport. Thus transport research provides knowledge about how movement takes place, how often, at what speed, and where (Taylor et al., 2001). Furthermore, an understanding of transport also provides knowledge about the barriers to transportation, such as its economic costs, or can identify whether and how other social indicators have the potential to make a difference (Bullard and Johnson, 1997).

This insight into the concept of transportation strongly emphasizes actual empirically traceable movement within given modes of transportation. The understanding is based on aggregating the individual behavior or movement of objects to investigate how transportation is conducted on a larger scale. This in turn has the potential to create analytical relationships between transport and different scientific themes, e.g., land use in relation to external spatialities (cities, regions, countries, continents), economic conditions (private economies, business models, state budgets), social groups (income, identity, gender, residency), or externalities (accidents, environmental impacts, economic activities). Transport thus represents an understanding of the actual traceable movements of people and objects and is therefore often understood through analysis that pairs quantified patterns of movements with external impacts on the system of transportation or externalities that are traced through their relationship to the system.

Mobilities

Mobilities research has emerged as a new approach to the study of transportation, viewing it as more than just a question of efficiently getting from point A to point B. While transport represents a material fact that can be investigated through quantified analysis, the recent rise of mobilities research suggests that the fact that we are moving should undergo further research to investigate the social and societal implications and meaning of movement. It is based on an understanding of modernity and mobility as being highly interconnected. Transportation is aiding the creation of a society on the move, which the social sciences need to investigate in new ways, with transportation being only one of several dynamics involved in this development. We are moving in more ways and over longer distances today than ever before and, according to the basic concept that underlies transportation, therefore also changing our relative status more often. Thus, transportation in mobilities research is understood in the way that it helps shape society, individuality, communities, and economies. Physical displacement, transportation is seen as just one way of moving because people, objects, images, and information are also moving through information and communication technologies (ICT). These new technologies help us overcome geographical distances in new ways, creating new borderless proximities, and because of this should be considered forms of mobilities, on a par with the physical displacement offered by transportation.

A decisive step in this direction was taken with Urry's (2000) book *Sociology Beyond Society – Mobilities for the Twenty-first Century*. Urry illuminates mobility as an integral component of modern societies through which they should be understood and analyzed. This argument is followed up and further developed in his 2007 book *Mobilities*. Different mobilities produce and reproduce social life and cultural forms, and it is in these mobilities that cultural patterns and identities are shaped and reshaped (Cresswell, 2006; Hannam et al., 2006; Sheller and Urry, 2006). Mobilities enable the composition of the many fragments and moments that everyday life consists of. In that way, mobilities make the late modern individual's autobiographical narrative possible, and the mobile individual copes with the various expectations of them by using a variety of practices and personal strategies (Bissell, 2019; Freudendal-Pedersen, 2009; Jensen, 2009; Kesselring, 2006).

The "mobilities turn" of traditional social sciences has given new perspectives to the idea of mobilities as "hidden" or "introvert" potential. This "turn" can be described as a conscious effort to open up the "black box" of traveling that has existed in social sciences. The mobility research field emphasizes a turning away from sedentary concepts and methods in the social sciences and a turning toward objects of analysis and methods that are adjusted to mobilities as the dynamics in society that should be investigated. This entails both an ontological and a methodical counterpoint to static social sciences, a call for a new analytical focus that investigates the interconnectivity between people and places (Adey et al., 2014; Hannam et al., 2006). This involves a recognition that people, places, and institutions are connected in many ways and that these connections are decisive for the way society develops. Uncovering why these mobilities take place, how they are carried out, and the consequences the mobile practices have for people, places, and ecosystems, it is vital to understand that mobility is not just an occurrence, or a connection between people and places, it is a force that is creating new ways of organizing society, supplying tools for shaping the identities of individuals, and impacting our ecosystems in the process (Adey, 2009).

qMobility research is interdisciplinary and covers a wide range of theoretical and empirical fields. Urry (2007, pp. 10–11) lists 12 main mobility forms, ranging from "migration" to "visiting friends and relatives." This list shows the variety of purposes associated with mobilities. Moreover, there are also empirical fields still relevant to understand these purposes but where materialities are the main focus. Some of these fields could be: information and communications technology (de Souza e Silva and Sheller, 2014; Kitchin and Dodge, 2009), politics and planning (Freudendal-Pedersen and Kesselring, 2016; Jensen et al., 2020; Pucci and Vecchio, 2019), the transportation of goods (Birtchnell, 2016; Cidell, 2012), and tourism (Hannam, 2016; Obrador-Pons et al., 2009) all from both global and local perspectives. Thus mobilities research stems from many different traditions and includes a vast array of different approaches. In the last 20 years, a large number of anthologies have been published in an effort to show the formation of mobilities paradigms and their variety, e.g., *The Ethics of Mobilities–Rethinking Place, Exclusion, Freedom and Environment* (2008); *Tracing Mobilities: Towards a Cosmopolitan Perspective* (2008); *Mobility and Locative Media: Mobile Communication in Hybrid Spaces* (2014); *The Routledge Handbook of Mobilities* (2014); *Exploring*

Networked Urban Mobilities (2018); *Material Mobilities* (2019); *The Routledge Handbook of Urban Mobilities* (2020); *Handbook of Research Methods and Applications for Mobilities* (2020) and many more.

Much of the sociological research concerning mobilities has centered on the automobile. This is partly due to the fact that this type of mobility is the clearest expression of the conquering of space, and partly due to the problems of pollution and risk. This has become more and more prevalent over time as car ownership and mileage have increased. In addition, the car has become a place where one feels at home and can relax. The car is no longer only a medium for coming to and from "home," it is a home in itself, a place for dwelling and for many, their social lives would be impossible without a car. The car has also come to function as a place where the individual can organize and do things previously done at home (Collin-Lange, 2013; Jensen, 2012; Laurier et al., 2008; Pearce, 2016).

A variety of methodologies to investigate mobilities

In 2009, John Urry and Monica Büscher were looking into the upsurge in research adapting the mobilities ontology. They discussed how a researcher's critical engagement through and in mobilities research shows how people, physically and socially, are part of making the world through their movements and the mobilization of people, objects, information, and ideas. In this way, researchers can play a role and make a difference to the ways in which mobilities are understood, not least in public policy. In this way, they were also calling for a response-ability from researchers (a point I will return to in Chapter 6) and underlining the importance of engaging with the empirical: "...there is no research and no social science without theory, but at the same time we argue that the mobilities turn folds analysis into the empirical in ways that open up new ways of understanding the relationship between theory, observation and engagement" (Urry and Büscher, 2009, p. 99). This engagement with the empirical can be found in many of the research approaches within mobilities. I will not be able to do justice to all of them but have chosen to focus primarily on the concept of motility.

Motility is not only about the actual movement, but also about the potential for mobilities. This approach deals with the individual's capacity to be mobile in relation to different forms of movement, and how this potential is activated and becomes resolved (Kaufmann, 2002, p. 37). In his book *Re-thinking Mobility*, Kaufmann (2002) develops the concept of motility and demonstrates a broader understanding of the relationship between the potentials for movement and actual movement. In more recent work, Kaufmann (2011) describes how cities can be understood and analyzed through the motilities represented by different regimes of transportation. This gives rise to a more nuanced view on the conditions for choosing movement, in a world with a vast and growing number of possibilities. As many sociologists have already noted, the western world is a world in which the knowledge of options and the skills to take advantage of these options are far more prevalent than ever before.

Understanding this potential for movement involves an integrated view of the circumstances combining an analytical view on institutional material arrangements with an analysis of certain social factors on an individual level. It is way of analyzing the conditions for being mobile, as a certain "mobile capital" (Kaufmann et al., 2004) that is tied to social circumstances. By characterizing the possibilities for movement, the notion of motility also characterizes the individual's capacity for engagement and the potential for changing their social status through a change of location or connectivity. Changing status from being part of a family, a working community, involvement in leisure activities or cultural communities, or traveling as a tourist are examples of different changes in social status, role, or identity, which are to varying degrees dependent on physical movement as a part of changes in social status. Consequently, these notions emphasize mobilities, in their plural forms, as an analytical gateway to a deeper understanding of social conditions and inequalities. Kaufmann's work on motility is related to the everyday movement in the Global North, whereas Sheller's (2018) book *Mobility Justice* frames these issues of inequality and class on a global scale.

With Kaufmann's concept, an analytical framework of mobilities emerges. He proposes an analysis of three different but highly integrated concepts: "access," "skills and knowledge," and "desires and aspirations" (Kaufmann, 2011; Kaufmann et al., 2004). This is an approach that is significantly inspired by practice research (Reckwitz, 2002; Schatzki et al., 2005; Shove et al., 2012; Spurling et al., 2013). The term "access" primarily deals with the temporal and economic barriers to undertaking a certain mode of transportation in a given environment. Temporally, access can be seen as the spatial distribution of infrastructure and options for transportation, in a given environment, relative to the distribution of people and their abilities to gain the necessary physical access to the options. The condition for using this option is a key indicator for access as well, most often investigated through the economic conditions for using the available transportation options.

Considered analytically as a quite distinct area but in many ways connected to access is the idea of "skills and knowledge," which represents the concept of the individual's abilities to use different forms of transportation. The distinction of skills goes in three directions: the physical ability to move one entity physically from one point to another; acquired skills, which are skills needed to act within the rules or regulation within specific forms of movement, such as a driver's license or the ability to read and understand a map; and the organizational skills to arrange one's own activities in such a way that abilities and skills are harmonized with the conditions and options for movement surrounding the individual.

The third concept consists of "desires and aspirations," which incorporates the act of taking possession of or utilizing options for transportation, and the values individuals attach to different modes of transportation. To know more about these processes, both the integration of heterogeneous values into the individual's own practice, such as "the freedom of the car," and the ability to establish a critical position toward one's own rationales are investigated. This analytical concept thus enters into a reflexive state where the individuals' own rationales behind their mobile practices can be paired with aspirations or dreams about a desirable reality. Leaving room for this reflexive space in between also opens up an opportunity to pair desires for motilities with broader aspirations and future plans held by individuals, such as sustainability, personal achievement, or development of their local community.

This context draws inspiration from transport research in terms of an interest in the conditions for individuals to engage in transportation systems. But while the analysis of user access to transportation systems has tended to focus on proximity in temporal terms and economic conditions, motility draws inspiration from the social sciences in order to focus also on the human capacities for appropriating different mobile technologies. In this way, the concept of motility is an attempt to place an analysis based on individual actual, experienced, and aspirational mobility into a context that describes the social significance of movement in space. It is very important to stress that these analytical categories in no way universally glorify more mobilities as the solution to social problems. The task of an analysis of motility is to investigate how potentials for mobilities materialize or are limited and how individuals take these potentials into their possession and integrate them into a narrative of their identity and aspirations. In that way, mobility has an ambivalence and an inherent inequality—an inequality which can also, but not only, be seen across social classes.

With this above understanding as a starting point, I will move to talking about sustainable mobilities as the horizon of change and what this can entail.

Knowledge as the pathway to a change toward sustainable mobility

Talking about sustainability can bring about many reactions. I hear from urban planning practitioners these days that it is a word that has gone out of fashion (this has happened a couple of times before, but it seems to be coming back). Academically, it has been criticized as a buzzword that removes politics from the climate agenda when the overall concept of sustainability is something everybody can agree on. This is because it does not address root causes of neoliberalism and its inherent inequality and thereby critical debate is annihilated (Swyngedouw, 2010). In line with this it is also criticized for being used politically, its function being to simulate an illusory global consensus that covers up global conflicts over distribution (Redclift, 1992) or remove the focus from the fundamental opposites of economic growth and protecting the environment (Sachs, 1993). The term "sustainability" is also used in many different contexts to signify very many different interrelated elements, some of which encompass relativistic notions of a certain balance between chosen entities over time. But sustainability has more to offer when it *can* be used to ask critical questions and point toward a goal for different futures. It can be used to ask if the current system can provide sustainable conditions for future generations, to question socio-technical aspects of the current transportation systems, and to ask whether those systems are reproducing and distributing unwanted social, economic, or environmental conditions detrimental to their long-term sustainability (Egemose, 2011).

Sustainability is also a call for transdisciplinarity, as no single research area can alone analyze and change the political and societal conditions for such wide-ranging conditions. Transdiciplinarity emphasizes a focus on the problem, and the problem is the starting point for finding relevant disciplines that can be used to understand and find possible solutions to the problem. What it underlines politically is the necessity for different research approaches within the same empirical field and with differences in geographies. There is a difference between the Global North and the Global South in the context of free and equal opportunities in mobilities, but the underlying ontology of the system it is based on is comparable. Taking the institutional material arrangements as a starting point, it becomes clear that mobilities have disadvantages as well as advantages and that it is a transforming element in societal terms. With sustainable mobilities, cooperation between research fields is the only way to address some of the complex societal, social, and environmental risks we are facing today

In times of pandemic we can turn back to research showing that being socially mobile is possible without the need for physical co-presence (Freudendal-Pedersen and Kesselring, 2021; Jensen, 2021; Salazar, 2021). This adds to the need for integrative approaches, not only in the distribution, planning, and organization of activities and infrastructure, but also in the theoretical framework presented by researchers to understand the current social reality. To understand the networked character of (urban) mobilities requires a move away from academic silos treating transportation as if it was not affecting its surroundings. It should be obvious from the previous pages that concepts to understand and plan mobilities often process inherently different scientific philosophies. Using models to predict and provide travel flows in order to regulate traffic systems or create new transport systems uses significantly different methods than analyzing the practices of mobilities in a cosmopolitan world. The above concept in depth describes different aspects of the mobilities system, from the physical trajectories paving the possibilities for mobility to the emotional and cultural affirmations in living the good life.

This approach to sustainability might be seen as slightly naive but, in the light of climate change and its consequences, there is increasing pressure to come up with alternatives to the current system. In both the EU and UN, it is increasingly strongly recognized that the current car-centered resource-intensive transport systems are not sustainable. In Denmark, new socioeconomic calculations have been used as a tool to underpin this, delivering results that show the cost of the current system. One kilometer by car costs society 0.32 DKK, while cycling generates 10.47 DKK and walking 21.49 DKK in benefits per km (Danish Technical University, 2018). The space required for a car is 140 m^2 at 50 km/h and 20 m^2 while parked. A bike uses 5 m^2 in motion and 2 m^2 parked (von Essen et al., 2018). Every kilometer driven by car produces a minimum of 258 gr of CO_2, compared to 22 gr for a high-end e-bike, and 0 gr for walking (Philips et al., 2020). Therefore, a policy of increasing—or even maintaining—car use flies in the face of national and European sustainability targets of 70% CO_2 reductions by 2030.

Accordingly, sustainable urban planning is a prudent strategy to combat these pressing challenges, when a city has the opportunity for common sustainable infrastructure in relation to water, energy, waste, heat, and—not least—transport. It is still an open question whether urbanization and its mobilities will continue to grow in the aftermath of the pandemic and there has been much speculation on this matter (Adey et al., 2021; Bereitschaft and Scheller, 2020; Campisi et al., 2020; Mell and Whitten, 2021). Nevertheless, what was already on the agenda prior to the pandemic has been highlighted in a time of drastically reduced physical mobilities. Good public space—living space—is of great importance for the people who live in and use a city and has a significant impact on whether we feel at home and comfortable there. Infrastructure and transportation create and define city spaces as traffic determines which cityscapes we have access to and how they can be used. This applies to all types of infrastructure projects. Most obvious are roads, each day filled by a growing number of cars making life increasingly difficult for cyclists and pedestrians and affecting the desirability of areas as places to live as well as the inequality for those who have to live there. One issue that the COVID-19 pandemic highlighted is the space occupied by parked cars which then become dead outdoor spaces. What has now become a more prominent item on the agenda is that while the car does provide freedom, it forces structures upon the city that lead to unintended consequences, creating unfreedom. Think about how many parents have the extra responsibility in an already time-pressured everyday life of chauffeuring their kids around. The problem with the close connection between freedom and mobilities is that it is based on a value system created by modernity and maintained through the right to free movement, which today is considered a fundamental right (Freudendal-Pedersen, 2009; Sennett, 1977; Urry, 2004). It has produced a system that is so strongly embedded and reinforced, not least through car commercials, that it seems impossible to also talk about all the unfreedom arising from automobility.

Car commercials often center around speed (and therefore freedom) of movement and the speed of movement has evolved to be a key factor in determining the arrangement of the world (Virilio, 1998). Urry (2000) talks about increasing speed as that which creates instantaneous time that is characterized by simultaneity and fragmentation. With this perception of time, constant development becomes the key word and stopping and slowing down is only for those with no other opportunities. Urry (2000) places instantaneous time in opposition to the clock time that organizes everyday life, forced upon us by industrialization, as an expression of synchronization and measurement of time. The climate change agenda and the COVID-19 pandemic are factors that have empowered the voices speaking against this speeding up of time. It is no new thing that individuals suffer under this constant speeding up. The dramatic rise in stress-related illnesses and the juggling of clock time—that still define day-care institutions and the working hours of many —have for more than a decade now been on the agenda. A change toward sustainable mobilities is also a discussion of the understanding of time. It is an understanding of which pockets of time can be slowed down and what they can be used for. Sennett (2007, p. 290) argues that the cities of the second modernity lack a sense of time, "...not time looking backward nostalgically but forward-looking time: the city understood as process, its imagery changing through use, an urban imagination image formed by anticipation, welcoming surprise."

Inviting surprises might be one of the biggest challenges for the future of urban mobilities. The technological fix often ends up being the agreement when it comes to imagining sustainable mobilities futures. The autonomous car is a good example of this. Let me say from the beginning that I see this technology having significant potential in public transport services and between urban areas, but the Human City and the autonomous car do not work well together. The technology is fascinating and has a large number of potential opportunities, but the fascination often seems to overlook the small things that matter to people. From a technocentric perspective, the automated car provides new and fantastic opportunities; it works in exactly the same way as an ordinary car except that transport time becomes your own personal time. Arguments for the automated car are therefore presented in line with the previous discussion on time and time pressure. I will return to this discussion in Chapter 6.

Conflict is needed

With the traditional viewpoint on the future role of the car strongly represented in politics and planning, there is no easy way to move beyond this. What is currently taking place is a strong resentment against contemplating any kind of reduction in available space to facilitate the movement and storage of cars. Simultaneously there is also a strong pull toward creating livable human cities with green spaces for dwelling and, not least, rainwater mitigation which requires surfaces other than asphalt (depending on the policy in play). This is about who has the right to city space. The discussion on the right to the city initiated by Lefebvre (1991b) in his book *The Production of Space – the Urban Revolution* is mostly related to opportunities for marginalized social groups to reclaim their right to the city in the process of urban transformation. This is not directly related to mobilities, but mobilities play a large role in urban transformations. There is a difference in the distribution of and access to mobilities, and new urban developments are often privileged with many opportunities to move in different modes. Reclaiming space that today is used for facilitating the car is, despite political, national, and international goals, still a very conflictual matter. Very frequently, when these discussions deal with the everyday practice of mobilities, the discussion ends up being black and white. In Denmark, whenever suggestions are made (as they occasionally are) to make part of a city car-free on one or two Sundays per year, the immediate response is how this will cause disruption, make it impossible for the workforce to do their jobs, and have a negative impact on the economy. Written like this it might seem ridiculous, but this is what happens on social media whenever a suggestion like this appears. It highlights the enormous emotional and conflictual agenda autologic planning has installed. The discussion most often ends as two ideologies fighting each other—no cars at all or cars everywhere. As Lefebvre (1976, p. 12) says:

> ...ideology masks the production of new relations as much as the renewal of the old ones, by masking the various contradictions and the critical moment. Pollution or the fight against it, destruction or construction of the environment, zero growth, negative or positive growth, none of these problems has anything beyond a limited, topical interest unless the question of the renewal of the relations is involved. They cannot be called 'factors'. What matters is their interaction, as an ensemble.

With this quote in mind, it can be argued that the best way to change the current planning rationale is to take another path. The conflict between cars and no cars often seems so heated that the idea of using the car in a different way and to start out by replacing the many short trips with active green mobility gets no place in the discussion. Framing this discussion in the context of climate change, the amount of asphalt and the problems this entails, and the wish for livable cities with spaces for dwelling and communities, is another take on this discussion.

This is also an approach emphasizing that cities are not only what is within them: to a large degree they are produced by what flows through them. As well as the everyday life mobilities of the city's inhabitants, multiple mobilities such as moving workers, tourists, business travelers, goods, information, waste, and so forth make cities a vibrant and living environment. These mobilities produce and reconfigure meanings, identities, and cultures day by day (Bissell 2019; Bissell 2014). As Georg Simmel put it in the 1920s, we just see the (material) forms of social processes and dynamics. But in fact, the world is mobile and dynamic, ever changing, like the elements of a kaleidoscope. In other words, mobilities are the constituting forces shaping the world. Cities are the product of the interactions, the crossings, separations, and segregations of mobilities and flows metamorphosing from intended decisions about spatial and material structures.

The material forms of mobility-based modern societies, their transport infrastructure, are a particular source of intense and ongoing conflicts, which constantly erupt over proposals such as highways, airports, train stations, and bridges. What mobilities do societies need, what is a good (mobile) life, what is a livable and sustainable city, and similar questions emerge and infrastructures become reflexive. In the past they became reference points for conflicting discourses about the necessity for acceleration and the genesis of more and faster flows. For a long time the idea that more mobility and transport produce more growth, more welfare, and "better places" was taken for granted in modern planning, engineering, and world making. But in the mobile risk society, the concept of the "zero-friction society" is questioned and contested. In a phase of modernization where financing has become precarious, citizens of all social classes are afraid of being the losers from globalization. The unintended negative consequences of the speeding up of societies begin to dominate everyday perceptions and discourses, and the "more mobility argument" loses its legitimacy and power. Violent confrontations such as those around Narita Airport in Japan and Frankfurt Airport in Germany in the 1980s, the conflicts concerning the Oresund Bridge between Sweden and Denmark, and the confrontations around the Stuttgart 21 rail proposal in Germany concentrate peoples' fears and doubts and their resistance to transport megaprojects. In this way, such confrontations are part of a quest for alternative futures.

This underlines the fact that in any change it is important to be responsive to the values important to everyday life. Planning must respond to some of the needs and aspirations people have for the "good city" and creating this new picture is the job of planners, architects, researchers, and similar professions. This is where utopias still have an important function. We can call it "future vision" or use other words that we may be more comfortable with, but either way we cannot expect a direct transition to ideal planning with sustainable mobilities without also providing a framework to understand it within. This also means overcoming the idea that individuals only think rationally, in the economic sense of the term, when deciding on everyday mobilities. Remaking, recrafting, or replacing everyday life mobility practices needs to be responsive to the values, cultures, and emotions of everyday life. A clear image of what future we are aiming for also removes the heavy burden on individuals in terms of their personal responsibility to create sustainable mobilities in the future.

Vergragt and Brown (2007) highlight the significant role that governmental institutions and municipalities have in promoting this shift toward sustainable mobility through encouraging investment in sustainable infrastructure and making active involvement and communication between various stakeholders essential in the planning process. So far the best examples of this have occurred as a result of "Tactical Urbanism" where low-cost test scenarios inform long-term implementations (Lydon and Garcia, 2015). In Copenhagen, this has enabled reprioritizing the use of large neighborhood streets to give more space to cyclists, pedestrians, and urban dwellings rather than cars (Freudendal-Pedersen, 2020) (this will be discussed in more detail in Chapter 6). Another example of the move away from autologic in cities is the flowering of projects working toward realization of the 15-minute city, in many cases making use of tactical urbanism (C40 Cities Climate Leadership Group and C40 Knowledge Hub, 2021). Most interventions have happened rapidly as part of government responses to the dramatic changes in mobility patterns caused by the COVID-19 pandemic, although a few previous studies of data-driven approaches to 15-minute cities exist (e.g., da Silva et al., 2020). The basic idea behind the concept is to gather together functions (schools, libraries, shops, public institutions) within a 15-minute walking or biking radius and to deter the use of cars. Many functions today are located based on the availability of the car, taking for granted that this is the preferred mode for all trips, which in turn facilitates more car usage.

Mobilities and urban space are mutually dependent and a future sustainable mobilities system must create quality in both. Sometimes this entails conflict, but the following chapters focus on how taking communities, emotions, and utopias as a starting point might be a pathway to help people, planning, and politics to imagine what a different future could look like.

4   Communities on the move

I think people, in general, are oriented toward communities, that
we need communities. Some seek large communities, are very extro-
vert, and are part of many communities, while others seek smaller
communities[1]

Looking through the many interviews I have carried out on different aspects of mobilities and everyday life, the above quote exemplifies the thoughts that appear when asking about communities. The
ontological security needed in everyday life is related to being part of
communities, and communities always entail mobilities. In Bauman's
(2001) book on *Communities*, he writes at the very beginning of the
book: "Words have meaning: some words, however, also have a 'feel'.
The word 'community' is one of them" (Bauman, 2001, p. 1). Being
part of a community is not just an activity—it is an activity that is
related to a "feel" of an embodied experience of the making of meaning and ontological security. In my research on everyday mobilities,
many of the stories told are about the reasons for moving and the communities you move to or from. It is evident that being part of something together with others is essential for the making of meaning in
everyday life. This is also about values, about what matters to people.
In this chapter, this will be discussed with examples from interviews
collected over the last 15 years which show in different ways the significance of communities and how the interviewees understand what a
community is. The starting point applied here is to take seriously how
the interviewees understand communities and the values embedded
in their understandings. Sayer points out that "values have come to
be understood in a way that divorces them from what they are about"
(Sayer, 2011, p. 19). Separating values from what they are about, communities in this chapter, means risking overlooking the fact that while
the shape and form of communities may have changed, the feel and the
values are constant. This chapter is an explorative investigation into

DOI: 10.4324/9781003100515-4

communities proposing that they are (still) essential to value-creating practices in everyday life.

The range of communities changed

When Putnam wrote his book *Bowling Alone* in 2000, it soon became a classic on the collapse of communities and is frequently cited. His interest started because "more than 80 percent (of Americans) said there should be more emphasis on community, even if that put more demand on individuals" (Putnam, 2000, p. 25). Putnam's investigation points to the significance of the massive urban sprawl, meaning that people's primary activity where they live is sleeping, while activities such as working, leisure, and shopping take place elsewhere. This demands a significant amount of shuttling between different places with very little time left to engage in local communities. He uses the example of a local bowling club as a story of decline, a club that used to be the local meeting place but was no longer able to attract members. There is no doubt that mobilities, especially automobility, is one element pushing what Putnam calls "decline," but to be more precise, it is the decline of specific kinds of communities. As Wellman (1999, p. xiv) points out: "The traditional approach of looking at community as existing in localities—urban neighborhoods or rural towns—made the mistake of looking for *community*, a pre-eminently social phenomenon, in *places,* an inherently *spatial* phenomenon." Developments in communication and transportation technologies changed the shape of communities as we knew them, and the family car was a key element in why many scholars deemed community to be eroding. Putnam presents data on how, in 1990, the US had more cars than people able to drive them and that the car and the commute "are demonstrably bad for community life. In round numbers the evidence suggests that *each additional ten minutes in daily commuting time cuts involvement in community affairs by 10 percent...*" (Putnam, 2000, p. 213). That mobilities and the decline of communities are understood as closely connected is evident in research throughout the last decades, though it is not the mobilities as such, but the individualization that they bring about.

This can also be seen in Tönnies' (1957) seminal work on *Gemeinschaft* and *Gesellschaft*. Here he conceptualized *Gemeinschaft* as a community with social interactions constituted through village cultures, common religious practices, and family life with all its unquestioned tradition. He distinguished this from *Gesellschaft*, a society with indirect interactions constituted through the industrial society where human interactions were loose and regulated through contracts and exchange of capital. *Gemeinschaft* for him consisted of the spontaneous face-to-face interactions of small sedentary populations where communities emerged organically due to conditions of life and the sharing of responsibility among a closely interacting group of people. As he expresses it, the *Gemeinschaft* does not think about whether it *is*—it just *is* (Tönnies, 1957). This is what Giddens (1991), among others, means by a "traditional community," where who you married, what kind of job you held, and what kind of leisure activities you engaged in was decided by the community you belonged to, due to the limited possibilities of moving away (either permanently or on a day-to-day basis). According to Tönnies (1957), what changed was the ability to be mobile and the increasing interventions by city councils or planning authorities, features that appeared with the modernization of societies and increasing individualization (Beck, 2008; Giddens, 1991). In these discussions, which became increasingly common in the 1990s (the age of individualization), the discrepancy between individuality and community became a major topic and the idea that community was declining became a frequent assertion.

In Bauman's book on community, he goes as far as to say that "'community' stands for the kind of world which is not, regrettably, available to us—but which we would dearly wish to inhabit and which we hope to repossess" and that it "is nowadays another name for paradise lost" (Bauman, 2001, p. 3). In this thinking, the idea of community is one that is based on a traditional society where individuals have no other option than to confine themselves to the existing frameworks. Transport and communication technologies made it possible to compose everyday lives in new ways. The opportunity to seek meaning and construct a lifestyle fitting who we wanted to be became an opportunity but also an obligation. This meant that a previously unseen focus on the individual, their wishes, and their dreams for the good life became center stage. Work patterns and family life changed as a result of modernization: work could demand long commutes and was no longer necessarily infused with personal obligations, women entered the labor market, and institutions took over the responsibility of caring for children and the elderly. This created an intense pressure to work, and family life and other factors essential for the maintenance of local communities declined. The consequence that individuals could no longer rely on the collective comforts provided by tradition is part of the community decline narrative. That place-bound traditional societies also could be suffocating and limiting, might involve sexually assault or mental or physical abuse, and were very difficult to escape from often seems to be missing in the community/individualization discussion. Nevertheless, the idea that everyone belonged to a specific community was rarely questioned made the distinction between belonging or not belonging much clearer cut than it is today.

Simmel (1972) illustrated these pre-modern communities as concentric social circles where the center illustrated the individual's identity and belonging. The impact of rapidly increasing and expanding physical and virtual mobilities, accelerating time and expanding range, means that these have become intersecting circles, creating multiple identities in many communities in what Simmel (1972) frames as a centrifugal tendency (see Castells, 1996; Kesselring and Vogl, 2008; Larsen et al., 2006). This is what Giddens (1991) is pointing to when he describes how individuals inhabit several lifestyles. Different situations in everyday life demand or provide the opportunity to inhabit a lifestyle that fits the situation. The function of the lifestyle is to have a large number of choices taken for granted, thereby producing a manageable number of reflexive choices. The lifestyles are held together so that they create meaning within a life-politic that encompasses the individual's moral orientation. Tönnies wrote about *Gemeinschaft* and *Gesellschaft* in 1957 and 20 years of development in transportation and communication systems made Bell and Newby (1976) elaborate Tönnies' framework, extending it to society's interaction with communities through a distinction between three different kinds of community: the Topographical, referring to sharing geographical space; the Local, referring to sharing bounds through social groups and local institutions; and Communion, referring to having close personal ties, belonging, and warmth. Though broader in its scope, this also makes the immense pace and altering effect diverse technologies of mobilities have had on communities even more obvious. In a mobile world the Topographical no longer has to necessarily refer to a physical space. Sharing bonds with social groups does not have to be local and close, and personal ties and warmth can exist between people living in different parts of the world. The social network approach had already moved away from this focus on the small tight-knit neighborhoods or towns during the 1970s and instead focused on "...how relationships fit into a variety of patterns of social structure" (Wellman, 1999, p. xiv). The story of the decline of communities, however, did not end and well into the early years of the twenty-first century the idea that mobilities meant an erosion of communities dominated. Within mobilities research, studies related to communities focused on sedentary notions of how people dwell in communities, both virtually and physically.

Communities as necessary for human existence

Despite Bauman's (2001) view of communities as something unavailable, he also argues that communities continue to be necessary for humanity's existence and continuation and that it is a dependence that has remained largely unchanged over the centuries. This dependence was often sidelined in late-twentieth-century sociological research where the focus was on individualization and its consequences for society. The beginning of the twenty-first century has shown an increased acknowledgement of the omnipresent need for communities. Various mobilities, potential mobilities, and travel resources are forces that influence how local communities, and the sense of belonging, develop (Fallov et al., 2013; Jorgensen, 2010a).

Within a mobilities framework, understanding communities calls for an approach to communities as places as well as their intersecting routes. This chapter sets out to understand communities from the perspective of everyday life with all its (in)stabilities and routines, involving children, homes, friends, leisure, work, and the physical and virtual mobilities they entail. All these elements in everyday life are constantly challenged and influenced by the multi-scale character of social practices, identity formation, and social processes (Castells, 1996; Giddens, 2002; Ritzer, 2010). Communities with different functions are what makes it possible to navigate everyday life. That means maintaining old communities or continuously seeking new communities appropriate to the current life situation. Different life phases are no longer necessarily linear; moving away from home, getting an education, starting a job, or starting a family can be shuffled around and these phases of life often mean new or additional communities. Communities are emerging around many of the same dynamics as did traditional communities, because people are continuously looking for other beings, to create meaning around the dynamics that are transforming their lived experiences (Dewey, 1954; Lippmann, 1993/1927). Physical and virtual mobilities expand and sustain communities through local and virtual forms of sharing responsibility and life experiences, thereby creating meaning and security. Examples of this can be community gardens, political movements, groups for parents with twins, and so forth. Virtual mobilities provide the opportunity to engage with causes, people, interests, and needs that are easier to locate online. Communities initiated by virtual mobilities can develop into physical co-presence communities as expressed by the following interviewee:

> I am in this group, it is a meet-up app, for women. I started using it when I moved to Scotland alone, I didn't know anybody, so I signed up to the app. When I came back to Denmark, I missed the international community and I found this really cool app. It is just an app with maybe around 100 people. Not everybody is active. But there are a lot of events and we go to dinner or out for a drink or go to Tivoli, and you just sign up and go along and then you meet the same people again and again and create a community in this group.

The above quote is a good example of how a co-dependence of phys-ical and digital mobilities exists and is integrated into and entangled with everyday life. This creates a challenge because, if communities are not limited to those that have a physical presence, how do we decide whether or not a community *is* a community? And is it our role to do so?

In this book, I suggest another approach. Based on theoretical work on modern everyday lives and how these are handled, our starting point is the function of communities in relation to essential human needs in everyday life (in)stabilities (Bauman, 2001; Beck, 1997; Beck et al., 2003; Delanty, 2003; Giddens, 1991; Putnam, 2000; Tönnies, 1957). The focus is not on form, localities, or co-presence, although these can also be important. Instead, the search for communities starts by focusing on four aspects related to the function of the community: *shared responsibility*, covering both large-scale issues such as environ-mental crises and small-scale, everyday things, like healthy food for kids (Davis, 2010; Freudendal-Pedersen, 2014b; Shove and Walker, 2010); *exchange of life experience*, which recognizes current practices and guides future practices, for instance, how to connect everyday life through different modes of mobilities (Freudendal-Pedersen, 2009; Heller, 1995; Jensen, 2012); *continuity and meaning*, which connects today's practice with future practices, essential for living (Eriksen, 2001; Nixon, 2012); and *ontological security*, which provides individ-uals with the basic feeling of sense-making, that everyday life choices make sense of the bigger picture (Beck, 1997; Giddens, 1991; Heinlein et al., 2012).

With this starting point, understanding communities is focusing on how people feel about and in communities. It is their experience, their making of meaning that is at the center. It can involve different forms of presence, commitment, and intentionality that are simultaneously localized and continued at a distance, through physical and virtual mobilities. The idea is that people are continuously seeking for new communities to emerge around the very same dynamics as with traditional communities. This is not a dismissal of research emphasizing what Giddens (1991) calls "disembedding." In Durkheim's (1997) work, it is a focus on how human life is distributed in spheres of functionalized institutional set-ups based on contracts, while Weber (1978) discusses how instrumental and bureaucratic rationality is taking over the rules of social organization. These discussions illustrate how traditional communities changed and how much of the care work that was previously a major aspect of communities has been institutionalized. The aim is not to diminish this, but it does not equate to a finding that communities are eroding. Tönnies' (1957 focus was also on how traditional communities faced pressure from urbanization. The move to the anonymity of the city was and is still discussed in relation to the alienation and insularity that everyday life in urban environments entails; we see this in the studies by Simmel (1971), Goffman (1959), and more recently Jensen (2006) and Sennett (2003). The point here is that disembedding, institutionalization, and individualization did put pressure on the individual, eroding traditional communities and seeing the emergence of new ones.

The above diagnostic of communities is based on a response to an increased individualization where fragmentation, ambivalences, and risks make individuals and artifacts into objects of consumption. Bauman calls it a liquid life that "...means constant self-scrutiny, self-critique and self-censure. Liquid life feeds on the self's dissatisfaction with itself" (2005, pp. 10–11). While Bauman uses this to understand why communities are no longer available to us, it is also possible that this same individualization is exactly why new forms of communities emerge. The main function of communities is a constant even if the contours change. The virtual and physical mobilities make it possible to leave a community if it does not fit, what Savage et al. (2005) call "elective belonging," but that does not imply, as they point out, that all communities are temporary or based on conviviality. In Sayer's book *The Moral Significance of Class* (2005), he directs our attention to how social science researchers often focus on all the negative emotions in relation to lay normativity and morality. As a result, much research has been on the erosion of communities. Sayer points in his book to other emotions like good-heartedness, benevolence, compassion, and gratitude and argues that it: "... requires us to take lay normativity seriously, particularly regarding the ethics of everyday life, and attend to its content and internal rationales" (Sayer, 2005, p. 5). Sayer's project is a different one, but it exemplifies the focus of this book when approaching communities within a mobilities ontology. In the following, I will discuss four types of community based on examples from previous empirical work mentioned in Chapter 2. They are examples of communities where *shared responsibility, exchange of life experience, continuity and meaning*, and *ontological security*, alone or in combination, are where the feeling of belonging originates.

Local communities

Local communities might be what is closest to traditional communities. The local communities have changed because moving away or deciding not to engage and instead find other communities is a possibility. Nevertheless, dwelling in a specific context opens up the opportunity of either random or organized meetings that become significant, as Savage et al. (2005) and more recently Jørgensen (2010b) and Fallov et al. (2013) have shown. The quote below is an example of how communities emerge in local neighborhoods:

> Especially the community out here, I think it's important. It's been the whole time. There's a lot of kids in the area and some of their parents are actually my best friends. And that's because were just together and there's been a nice arrangement. Sometimes we meet at the playground, sometimes you take care of other people's kids in the playground. I call them road friends when I tell my other friends about them. They can't understand why we are so close, for others it might *just* be neighbors. It's been really nice to have this community here.

Everyday life with kids without a doubt plays a significant role in local communities. The everyday managing of kids demands organization, and keeping kids active at the weekend or on shorter bank holidays often involves the playground. The "spontaneous" meetings at the playground that recur again and again can turn it into a close community where members bring coffee, spend several hours talking and interacting, and look after other people's kids. Playgrounds connected to a smaller urban area very often have the same people returning repeatedly, creating the opportunity to pass the time or meet the parents of the children your kids are playing with. You *exchange life experience* of what it means to be a parent, or you *share responsibility* and can leave for a short while to handle other everyday business because you trust the members of the community. This provides *ontological security* and becomes a place where you feel safe. As the following quotes show, these communities can also be significant when the kids grow older and the playground is no longer part of everyday routines:

> It is the community we have. We have a road association where we have been cooking together for many years. It is not that often anymore because the kids got older, but I think we did a lot to grow the community.

Everyday life with kids is very often quite place bound, and this opens up the opportunity to take care of the local neighborhood, newcomers, or other types of care work like walking the dog for a sick neighbor. Other types of local communities are centered around sharing as exemplified by the following quote:

> We have these sharing rooms in our building where we share tools and furniture and all sorts of other things. It works really well. And we also have an exchange shelf where you leave stuff you don't need any more and other can just take it.

The argument here is not that a local neighborhood equals a community, but it is there, and it is significant. An important part of what (initially) holds them together is co-presence in the same way that traditional communities worked. When claims are made that people no longer have the time to engage in local communities, it might be because: "...post-modernist literature on identity has underestimated security needs, the desire for intimacy and informality, closeness, confirmation and recognition" (Eriksen, 2004, p. 138) [my translation]. Local everyday communities are still essential and have not lost their meaning. In 2002, a study was carried out that showed how proximity was still an essential factor in the formation and maintenance of friendships, and these are not only brief or superficial friendships, but friendships created through common history and experiences (Juul, 2002, pp. 168–169).

This does not mean that what Larsen et al. (2006) showed in their examination of networks where friends were scattered over large distances is not also part of life. Instead, it underlines the different needs in different life phases and for different situations. The organization of everyday life with children, work, and other caretaking and leisure activities needs local communities. This does not exclude other important friendships working through different, and probably often less practical, interdependence. When Lofland (1998) described the modern industrialized metropolis as a "city of strangers," reflecting ideas also put forward by Simmel (1971) and Goffman (1971), it is a focus on the city as a single large whole. When we see the city as composed of many small local communities, it is not strangers you meet. There are different degrees of familiarity and co-existence; not everything is a local community, but the view of the city is a question of scale. This question of scale might be part of the reason for the perceived erosion of communities. This resonates with the story Barry Wellman tells in the introduction to his book *Networks in the Global Village – Life in Contemporary Communities*. Growing up in the Bronx in New York, he was surprised when starting to study sociology "to find it full of concern about the supposed loss of community" (Wellman, 1999, p. xii). His experience from growing up in the Bronx was that ties to other people stretched far beyond the local neighborhood. This was a time without virtual mobilities, but people found ways to communicate outside the local scale.

Virtual communities

Virtual communities have been discussed as an essential player in community erosion because they offered opportunities to "escape" from local communities even when physically present or choosing not to engage at all. Empirical research findings over the last two decades have shown that virtual communities are maintaining old and creating new communities (Licoppe and Inada, 2010; Wellman, 2001; Wellman and Gulia, 1999; Wilken, 2010). Sometimes new virtual communities evolve into physical face-to-face meeting, which will be discussed in the next section as hybrid communities. In this section, the focus is on the communities that only exist virtually. Sometimes these communities are about finding kindred spirits where solidarity is the major attraction. With a virtual community, the search radius for *ontological security* enlarges and *shared responsibility* becomes possible as this example highlights:

> Right now I am very occupied with discussions on gender sexuality and equality. When you open up about this on Facebook or share something on Instagram it doesn't matter what the topic is, you become a participant in these pages. Here I feel like I am part of a community together with people who believe in something specific, and we stick together. And we also fight against that common enemy.

It seems that virtual communities have played a large role in creating different kinds of communities where ontological security can be found and in which the sharing of responsibility plays an important role in this creation process. For example, virtual communities played a major role in the growing strength of the #Metoo movement. The Fridays for Future movement (also known as School Strike for Climate) is another example. Kesselring (2008a, p. 20) argues that "Technology is social: it is a social process, not a finite product! Virtual spaces are not technological or even antiseptic spaces. They are dynamic, and they are spaces of social encounter and interaction between people living and working in very different places, contexts and cultures." This quote relates to Kesselring's investigation of mobility pioneers, people for whom work is to a high degree dependent on virtual co-presence and communities. These virtual communities can be long distance or in close proximity. Licoppe and Inada show in their research how friendships evolve in online games where the basic idea is to create a community of gamers in a specific game where their interaction is based on text messaging (Licoppe and Inada, 2010, p. 695). They show how there are behavior norms that depend on "...local sense-making practices, cultural constraints, and resources" and that these norms are specific to each community and form the framework for what it means to belong to this community and be a member (Licoppe and Inada, 2010, p. 698). Another highly interesting aspect of their findings is that proximity is part of the game: being in the same public space— maybe even on the same café—but only communicating through the virtual media. Meeting is a possibility, but it is not a necessity in order to be together and share an experience. This is the same kind of sharing experiences that the interviewee below relates to:

> There are also the Facebook communities. I am part of a photo group with people who live in the same area. It is really funny to see how people in your own neighborhood sees things. They take pictures from totally different angles, and you see a lot of different perspectives.

The photo community *exchange life experiences* by sharing their views of the neighborhood they are living in. They see different perspectives and also sometimes new perspectives. These virtual social meeting places play an increasingly large role in everyday life. Licoppe (2018) investigates this with empirical examples of meetings and dating. These virtual relations and encounters, he says, mean that "the city becomes less a 'place of strangers' than a place of discoverable 'pseudonymous strangers' with retrievable profiles" (Licoppe, 2018, p. 47). If you go on a date or just meet someone randomly, you are very likely to have searched them on social media before the date or that you do so when the random acquaintance goes to the bathroom. Along these lines, Kesselring shows in his work with mobility pioneers how various virtual "...technologies provide people with the (mobility) potential to substitute other modes of presence and absence, proximity and distance" (2008a, p. 35). Some of these virtual communities never move into co-presence, they stay purely virtual. Others become a mix where the virtual communities can have the same kind of significance as co-presence communities. In this way, they become simultaneously virtual and locally grounded, what are termed here "hybrid communities."

Hybrid communities

Today, virtual and physical mobilities often interact in the creation and maintenance of local communities. These hybrid communities can be initiated both locally or virtually and the different forums for meeting up and exchanging life experience support the maintenance of the community. When the internet became accessible to a majority of people, it was considered a threat to communities. Bauman's (1998) book on globalization describes how the development of information technology is dissolving the local because the "close community" of the past was "... brought into being and kept alive by the gap between the nearly instantaneous communication *inside* the small-scale community..." (Bauman, 1998, p. 15). But as exemplified in the section above, the opportunity to ask for help or support by reaching out to the virtual community is very often also related to interaction in the local community. This idea of the internet as destroying communities has also been rejected in the last decade:

> It is becoming clear that the Internet is not destroying community but is resonating with and extending the types of networked community that have already become prevalent in the developed Western world. Old ties with relatives and former neighbors are maintained; new ties are developed among people sharing interests (Wellman, 2001, p. 2032)

Examples of this can be searching for old friends on Facebook and meeting up again, an opportunity that before virtual mobilities would have demanded a lot of work. Other examples are relatives living in different countries who can have virtual face-to-face meetings and eat dinner together or celebrate birthdays. During the COVID-19 pandemic, this for many became the only opportunity to connect with close friends and family. Also, the more day-to-day interaction in communities can be a mixture of virtual and physical mobilities, as the example below shows:

> I am part of this community where we have a Facebook group to communicate with each other. Also, with the friends I have from my study we also have a small Facebook group where we talk about all that is difficult and also about the good things. We also make appointments on Facebook to see each other physically but most of the immediate difficult things we also talk about just on Facebook.

In this way, the virtual part of the hybrid communities offers a place to share and be open about difficult situations. It becomes a safe space where difficult discussions can be opened up. Through these discussions *continuities and meaning* in relation to handling being a student with all its social and intellectual challenges are created. The virtual part of the community seems here to be the place where most of the difficult situations are discussed and a *shared responsibility* for how to handle difficult situations is created. In Thomas Hylland Eriksen's (2004) book on communities, he also points to how the virtual maintains the local:

> Although the internet is potentially borderless and placeless, nothing is automatic. Most individuals, on the contrary, seek the safe and well known, which confirms rather than challenges their existing world structures. The internet is there as a supplement, or an extension, to existing social ties and networks, not instead of them (Eriksen, 2004, p. 137) [My translation].

This is not to say that the internet cannot play a role in taking attention away from the local community, but the communities of today are so much more than just the local. *Continuity and meaning, shared responsibility, exchange of life experiences,* and *creating ontological security* do not only happen when people are physically face-to-face. It is understandable how these discussions on eroding communities came about in the wake of the increasing focus on individual choices and the need to create individual lifestyles and life politics (Giddens, 1991). The traditional community was based on lifelong projects, and in modern communities this is no longer always the case. According to Bauman (2001), this means that the ties we have with others in the same situation are fragile. However, what this chapter points out is while they are replaceable if they no longer fit, they can also be lifelong and strong.

Communities in physical mobilities

The last type of community I will discuss is communities in physical mobilities. This is of specific interest in relation to the discussion of planning mobilities in Chapter 3. Within the technocratic transport planning paradigm, travel time is considered wasted or dead time. That this is not the case has been developed through empirical research where the quality of time in mobilities as free or "own" time is emerging, as this interviewee expresses: "When you get into the car or train, bus, metro, you perhaps just need to relax and be on your own, disconnect mentally and concentrate on yourself." When Putnam (2000) described the erosion of communities, the "in-between" spaces, to use Urry's (2000, p. 141) term, that physical mobilities offer are not considered in his work. This is very likely because of the empirical setting for the research where the individual car was center stage. The car is a technology that is designed for individuality, this also comes out in the interviews:

> Unfortunately, I think, and I have seen this, that even if people are part of a cycling community, the minute they get a car, then they are lost, because then egoism steps in. It does, I tell you.

It might be egoism, which is what the interviewee blames in the above quote, but research also indicates that the car is a personal space, possibly the only space where many people today have alone time, a private space where intimate conversations with close friends or family can be shared (Conley and McLaren, 2012; Featherstone, 2004; Freudendal-Pedersen, 2009; Urry, 2006). One interviewee once told me that the only place she could have serious conversations with her kids about the loss of their father (who died from cancer) was in the car. The confined space where nobody was intruding and eye contact was not possible created a perfect space for having difficult conversations. In this example, the car provided the same safe framework as Facebook did for the student talking to her fellow students about the difficulties in their education. The car is a private space, but also very often functions as a social place where close communities are created or maintained: "When you were 18 you lived in the car, it was a community with all your friends, it was real freedom." This is an example of liminal small-group communities that exist in the "in between" spaces of mobilities that are important in people's lives (Urry, 2000, p. 141 see also Jensen, 2012).

As the first quote in this section mentions, cycling can mean being part of a community. This can be because of a cycling culture, or it can be the opposite where the community is based on resistance. In the following quote, it is a cycling culture that produces the community feeling:

> It always makes me happy when I meet one of the digital cycle counters telling me that I am number 1324 passing by on a bike today. Then I can tell I am part of a bigger movement. It is just like climate change; the important thing is to make people feel that they are a part of a bigger project. It indicates that you are making a difference.

In this example, it is clearly the *shared responsibility* and the *continuity and meaning* that are in play. The next quote relates to the *ontological security* that comes from the feeling that everyday life practices make sense as part of the bigger picture:

> The best thing about Copenhagen is that there are so many people who are used to cycling. They create a special flow; sometimes it is almost poetic when everybody knows what to do and how to behave. When the flow is working it gives an atmosphere of a very carefree life, for instance when you can see millions of cyclists waiting for the green light and then they start moving and it is the kind of movement where everybody knows what to do – that's beautiful.

These examples are about individualized mobilities where communities emerge as a result of doing "the same" as others, being part of a bigger movement that creates meaning. This also comes out in relation to public transport: "It's this thing about being able to sit and read on the train. And it's also cozy to look at other people when you take the metro. There is a great city feeling about taking the metro, and you can bring the newspaper. I like that; it's very cool." Some communities are formed when collective modes of mobilities are used. Here an interviewee is talking about the importance of the everyday encounter:

> We have what we call the morning team at the station where I live. We have always met each other at the station and said "Good morning" and stuff like that. So, I have a lot of contacts. So, every time I go to the station there are at least one or two I know. It is this kind of small community where almost everybody knows each other.

Again, *continuity and meaning* comes into play here. Hanne Louise Jensen (2012) shows in her research how communities develop through traveling together, how being part of the same commute changes fellow commuters from what Ole B. Jensen (2010), inspired by Goffman, calls a "mobile other" into a "mobile with." They meet in the same train every morning and use their commute to *exchange life experiences* and develop a community where they take care of each other. Jensen also researches the commuting communities in cars where the same kind of *sharing of life experience* and *continuity and meaning* are essential elements in these communities in physical mobilities.

Communities on the move

Based on the four types of mobilities described above, communities on the move are related both to how communities are in a constant process of development and also the interconnection between virtual and physical mobilities and communities. The question has been raised within the mobilities paradigm if the word "communities" needs to be replaced so that it can capture the mobilities that communities entail (Kaufmann, 2002; Urry, 2000). The term "networks" was already there as a way of understanding interdependencies and contemporary forms of patterned interaction (Castells, 1996; Larsen et al., 2006; Rainie and Wellman, 2012; Wasserman and Faust, 1994; Wellman, 1999). Barry Wellman in particular carried out empirically based research on social networks as a way of understanding the communities of today: "Although community was once synonymous with densely knit, bounded neighborhood groups, it is now seen as a less bounded social network of relationships that provide sociability support, information, and a sense of belonging" (Wellman, 2001, p. 2031). Using social network analysis, he has been investigating and reconnecting individuals to relationships and understanding how these relationships are embedded in specific ways. This research emphasizes that communities have not been eliminated or destroyed, that the support entailed in communities still exists, and that the traditional close-knit neighborhood community is just one form of community (Wellman, 1999).

Within the mobilities paradigm, Sven Kesselring has used social networks to understand how journalists and industry workers living in networks "... gives life to it [the network]. Switching between national territories and continents, he has given up his former goal to marry and to start a family. Love, sex, and friendship follow the idea of networking" (Kesselring 2008b, p. 29). The social networks describe life in a time where multiplex national and international networks define a space for living and working. The term "networks" highlights the flow in the diverse technologies that manage communication and transportation and the fluidity of various kinds of relationships, where stability, coherence, and embeddedness can be present. As Kesselring (2008b, p. 20) describes it: "Networks define the spaces and places where we live and where we work. They connect important places and people in the world, they create connectivities and communicativeness."

Another concept, originally coming from art, is the concept of assemblages, whereby social assemblages are defined as "a set of human bodies properly oriented (physically or psychologically) towards each other" (DeLanda, 2006). The focus here is on the idea that meaningful social analysis must focus on social entities on all scales without any assumptions about the form of functional unity. It is often used as a way to understand relations between materials, social processes, and semiosis/coding. The idea is that each component in an analysis can be unplugged from one connection and plugged into another without losing its identity. In other words, there is no fixed link between the components and each component is self-sufficient.

The concept of assemblages is a way of breaking away from ideas anchored in traditional communities where the individual is nothing on its own. In Lauren Wagner's (2018) work, changing the perspective from humans-as-static into understanding humans-as-moving involved a need to assemble the mesh of all the institutional, material, and political elements at play. Through this assembling "...I observed a sense of belonging that happened in mobility, specifically in interaction with like-minded (yet diverse) others who were viscously engaged in parallel assemblings of leisure consumption practices" (Wagner, 2018, p. 66).

The two concepts of networks and assemblages have been used intensively during the last two decades but have also been criticized.

In Couldry and Hepp's (2017) book *The Mediated Construction of Reality*, they discuss communities (they use the word "collectives") in a society dominated by virtual mobilities: "We define as a collectivity *any figuration of individuals that share a certain meaningful belonging that provides a basis for action – and orientation-in-common*" (Couldry and Hepp, 2017, p. 168). By relating the title of their book to Berger and Luckmann's *The Social Construction of Reality* (1966), they underline the making of meaning as essential. This drives their critique of the concepts of networks and assemblages, criticizing the network concept for falling short "...of understanding the overall constructions of meaning that *orientate* human action" (Couldry and Hepp, 2017, p. 61) and the assemblages concept for saying very little "...about the type of 'coming together' involved" (Couldry and Hepp, 2017, p. 62). The critique is based on how collectives have expanded through the everyday use of virtual technologies. The boundaries are blurry but what is essential is the collectives's need to create meaning and share responsibilities (Couldry and Hepp 2017, pp. 169–170).

What the discussion of these concepts highlights is that an understanding of communities on the move requires concepts that embrace the specific research agenda. With a focus on the mobilities practices of everyday life where life experience can be exchanged and ontological security is created (Bauman, 2001; Beck, 1997; Giddens, 1991), communities that are locally bound or mobile with intersecting routes matter and they make a difference. As mentioned at the beginning of this chapter, the word "community" has a "feel." This "feel" tells us something about what matters to people, and these elements are an important driver of change.

Communities as drivers of change

In Beck's book *The Reinvention of Politics* (1997), he discusses how in a risk society political discussions and divisions of responsibilities have changed and the individual is taking a leading role creating their own "subpolitics." The traditional political forums can no longer guarantee security, leading to the politicization of formerly non-political areas such as everyday life, work life, and leisure, which Beck terms "subpolitics." Subpolitics does not necessarily happen in an organized way, but it is a pervasive element in our practices, and we are often not aware that we are acting subpolitically (Beck, 1997). Where life politics is made up of individuals' choices and moral issues (Giddens, 1991), subpolitics deals with where in society consensus is arrived at on various topics. Both concepts have individualization as a starting point, where individuals have to define themselves through life politics and subpolitics. An important difference is that the concept of subpolitics involves an interplay with more established (sub)political institutions where responsibility can be shared with a community, rather than resting with the individual (Beck, 1992). This means communities become drivers of change: "[when] people become inhabitants of new virtual communities this may usher in something of a new 'global civic society'" (Rheingold, 1994, p. 265 as quoted in Urry, 2000, p. 73). Fridays for Future is a good example of this. It is a manifestation of subpolitics that virtual mobilities transformed into a large international community. Fridays for Future is a community on the move who made possible a new "community of fate" (Urry, 2000, p. 203) driven by a need to share responsibility for a global/local issue. This also highlights how "Sociotechnical and cultural developments in mobile communication and communicative mobility are not just of interest to a small elite, for they are effecting powerful changes in the entire urban, regional, and global fabric of spaces of public and private life" (Sheller, 2004, p. 43). Subpolitics is the opportunity to work on a global scale where a common language is found:

If one, in addition, has a common project, a goal for the future which is dependent on the other group members' efforts to succeed, it helps tremendously. And furthermore, if one can name a common enemy, someone else who threatens to thwart the plans, then everything is laid out for a strong and solidarity we-feeling which lasts as long as it is possible to identify that enemy... (Eriksen, 2004, p. 63) [My translation].

Communities on the move offer a much larger opportunity to seek out connections where *responsibility can be shared* in relation to issues that would otherwise lead to paralyses of action. Where traditional communities were often understood as limiting freedom, Bauman (1988) underlines how they also created freedom because they limited the number of choices that had to be made. Freedom is also an important part of being in contemporary communities, not because they limit the number of choices, but more in relation to *sharing responsibility* and *continuity and meaning* as this interviewee expresses:

If you can see the happiness of being in some communities, it also creates a freedom. For me, I think, it's closely linked with the feeling that I can do something together with other people. This thing about being able to do something with other people is also very closely linked to the feeling that you can be useful for something, to feel that other people need you. This is a feeling we all need because we don't function as humans if we cannot feel that other people need us in some sense.

This quote can be read as highlighting a tension between communities and individualization where a community is something that is consumed whenever it fits the purpose and abandoned when needs are no longer being fulfilled. Another reading is that it highlights the importance of communities for ontological security and the making of meaning, for feeling happy. This is about the emotions that are significant drivers for everyday practices and that we might have neglected to take seriously enough, as Sayer suggests:

> Emotional responses to the inequalities and struggles of the social field and how people negotiate them are to be taken seriously both because they matter to people, and because they generally reveal something about their situation and well-being; indeed, if the latter were not true the former would not be either (Sayer, 2005, p. 37).

In the following chapter the focus will be on the significance of emotions in relation to a change toward sustainable mobilities. Sustainable mobilities is a new ordering of the institutional material arrangements that are increasingly taken for granted. Imagining how this might look needs stories, visualizations, and utopias to create a horizon for change. The emotional responses to or wishes for possible futures are essential for making those futures happen.

Note

1. Unattributed quoted material is taken from my various interviews as described earlier in Chapter 2

5   Emotions and utopias

The previous chapter focused on the role of communities and the "feel" associated with them. In this chapter, the focus will be on how emotions, ascribing significant meaning to elements of everyday life, are an important driver for change. Utopias are, so to speak, a visualization of these emotions. They tell us something about what matters to us and what we don't like. The issue of climate change might be discussed scientifically with a focus on technical issues, but the way people react to it is emotional What kind of world are we leaving to our kids? What consequences does my consumption have for extreme weather events around the world? In relation to everyday mobilities, it is accepted knowledge that cars constitute a major issue. The following quotation shows the inherent guilt produced by this knowledge: "Now I have a car using leaded gasoline, and one feels guilty driving it... a little bit...but it is not just me doing it. I also have a friend who drives a car with leaded gasoline; I think that is really stupid. I would like to get a car which drives on non-leaded gasoline." Guilt is not productive when it comes to changing practice, guilt produces ambivalence and thus increases the need for structural stories that sustain current practice. The knowledge that there is an environmental issue in relation to car driving has not so far resulted in any change and that there is no direct link between knowledge and action is not a new issue. Also, it is extremely likely that the comments in the interview quoted above were triggered by the interviewer's specific research focus, sustainable mobilities. For the interviewee, it becomes a moral issue when reflecting on everyday practices. Bauman (1995) argues that the responsibility for acting morally correctly falls back on the individual when individualism entails no collected societal ethics with rules for what is correct. Instead, moral issues enter the routinized everyday life, and in relation to the issue of sustainable mobilities, it seems not to have a large impact on practices.

DOI: 10.4324/9781003100515-5

This does not mean, however, that changes are not wished for, but the specific change in practice is difficult to imagine. Therefore, imaginaries of how everyday living without a car could look like become of the utmost importance. In his 1984 book *Everyday Life in the Modern World*, Lefebvre stresses the importance of lived lives and their ability to transform. He underlines the importance of utopian thinking:

> And why not? For me this term has no pejorative connotations; since I put all the emphasis on adaption; since I refute "reality," and since for me what is possible is already partly real, I am indeed a utopian; you will observe that I do not say utopist; but a utopian, yes, a partisan of possibilities. (Lefebvre, 1984, p. 192)

It is the possibilities this chapter wants to investigate. How can we imagine different layouts of the urban so that facilitating automobility is no longer the first priority in planning and policy? The impact the car has on urban space is not a new realization. The Situationists movement was formed in 1957 by avant-garde artists, political scientists, and intellectuals, inspired by Marxism, and put forward a critique of mid-twentieth-century advanced capitalism (Pinder, 2020). Among other things, they focused on the impact of future cities dominated by cars and, to give one instance, created models of future cities exclusively centered around parking lots (Sadler, 1998). The idea behind these creations was to initiate change by exposing the rationales and logic of the capitalist order. "The breaking up of the dialectic of the human milieu in favor of automobiles... masks its irrationality under pseudopractical justifications" (Laclan in Sadler, 1998, p. 25). With their work, they produced a critique focusing on the alienation with which capitalist society has infused all areas of life and its exclusion of—among other things—emotions and experiences (Pinder, 2020; Plant, 2002). One example of pseudopractical justifications for cities being dominated by an autologic is the close connection between cars and growth. That this connection is far more complicated and based on specifically chosen correlations has continuously been discussed (Eddington, 2006; Litman, 2006; Sachs et al., 2007). However, it still remains a recurring issue in the (social) media whenever any kinds of restrictions on cars are discussed publicly.

Today, despite a growing focus on transportation's impact on climate change, solutions to car congestion are often sought by building new roads. Despite new socioeconomic models showing that many strategies and visions working together are imperative to avoid ending up in a vicious cycle of ever-widening roads, and the Intergovernmental

Panel on Climate Change emphasizing that avoiding (car trips) and shifting (modes) go hand in hand with electrifying the car fleet, it seems the autologic is unchangeable. A rationale exists that allows bottlenecks in the transport system to be perceived only as technical problems, which means a systematic growth and manifestation of the car as the only possible type of everyday life mobility (Freudendal-Pedersen, 2009, 2020). In this chapter, the main idea is to leave aside the issue of climate change, which often produces guilt (as in the above example), and instead focus on the right to the city. Through this perspective, it becomes possible to focus on the positive emotions related to the form and shape of everyday life in future cities. This discussion was initiated by Lefebvre (1996, original version in 1968) in his book *Le droit à la ville* (*The Right to the City*). In this book, Lefebvre focused on marginalized groups in the process of urban transformation, discussing the opportunities to make claims in relation to struggles over urban space as part of political decision-making. Focusing specifically on cars, Peñalosa (2008, p. 313) writes: "Cars parked on pavements and parking bays carved where there should be pavements are symbols of a democratic deficit and a lack of human dignity. It shows that the needs of citizens with a car are considered more carefully than those of people who walk." The car's occupation of urban space and its consequences for the everyday is an ongoing discussion, with Jane Jacobs (1961) as an important inspiration.

However, the logical positions resulting from this discussion seem unable to affect the extent to which a "logical" connection between cars and growth has come to be generally accepted and unquestioned. The Situationists discussed this as a struggle between "imaginations" and "common sense" in which capitalism's structure creates what Marx (1976) called false consciousness and Berger and Luckmann (1966) described as reification. These terms outline different scales of reproduction of practice and institutional material arrangements; individuals are not even aware they reproduce. It illuminates how individuals understand living within specific frameworks or structures that limit the possibilities for doing anything different from what they are doing. One of my favorite quotes from an interviewee on this is the following:

We are subordinated to some mechanisms, this goes for the car, the computer and technology—we can't say no to them. In some ways they force themselves through and shape our society. Cities and togetherness are formed by cars. One must not fool oneself into believing this is under democratic control, we have as much influence as the potatoes had on whether they wanted to become widespread in Western Europe. Cars are not something that man has, they are a socio-cultural unit which has man—cars have a life of their own.

This quote shows the need to make an overall structure or system (or structural story) to take away the responsibility because thinking about everyday life organization without the car it is simply not possible. The car's dominant role as that which connects everything means guilt is not an efficient strategy. Instead, the argument is that what is needed is utopias or visions of futures in which the emotions of everyday life are taken into consideration. Here, inspiration can be drawn from the Situationists who saw their work in the city as a "revolutionary potential of their own tactic of creating 'situations' as opposed to what they saw as Lefevbre's more passive stance of experiencing 'moments' when they happened to arise" (Sadler, 1998, p. 45). An example of this is the 1965 White Bicycle Plan by the Amsterdam-based group Provo, where hundreds of bikes were collected, painted white, and placed around Amsterdam for anybody to use for free. The bicycles disappeared after a while, one story saying they were removed by the police because maintenance was not considered and broken bikes were lying around (Sadler, 1998, p. 26). This "situation" became an inspiration to create what is known today worldwide as shared urban bike systems. How planning can play a role in creating situations that can visualize and inspire new ways of organizing everyday life, I will return to this later in this chapter and also in Chapter 6. First, the focus will be on taking emotions seriously and understanding them as part of urban utopias and planning.

Emotions in everyday life

With everyday lives as the epistemological starting point for research, the creation of meaning and significance—why things matter to people (Sayer, 2005, 2011)—comes out in the interviews. Everyday life is very practical, but is also influenced by sometimes abstract conceptions of time, freedom, and community. Emotionally influenced practice is also related to the four elements used to search for communities in Chapter 4: *sharing responsibilities, exchange of life experiences, continuity and meaning, and ontological security.* The topic of emotions is embedded in the mobilities ontology and within the field growing research on what is conceptualized as "affective mobilities" has shown the importance of what happens to the bodies on the move. "These 'affective mobilities' cover a wide range of topics and processes. They consider, for example, the role of affect in triggering and accompanying movement as well as in settling down and building a sense of home and of belonging to a place and community" (Glaveanu and Womersley, 2021, p. 2). Mobilities research has developed the understandings of embodied and sensory experiences as essential factors playing a role in shaping the institutional material arrangements and practices of mobilities. These embodied and sensory experiences go beyond the "rational" time- and money-oriented thinking that traditionally guides transportation research (Cass and Faulconbridge, 2017).

The traditional rational starting point views emotions as an "irrelevant accompaniment," but as Sayer (2011, p. 39) puts it: "emotions are not merely an irrelevant accompaniment to what we are doing, like muzak in a supermarket, but a kind of bodily commentary on how we, and our concerns, are faring." The quotation comes from Sayer's book *Why Things Matter to People* (2011) where he confronts social sciences with the difficulties they have in acknowledging that feelings are "...matters of 'practical reasons,' about how to act..." (Sayer, 2011, p. 2). To exemplify how this approach differs from the theoretical and empirical questions social sciences usually ask, he uses an example from Renato Rosaldo's book *Culture and Truth* (1989). In this book, Rosaldo describes the tragic death of his wife as an opening toward understanding the significance of emotions. He explains how "anthropologists writing about the ways in which cultures deal with death did so 'under the rubric of ritual rather than bereavement,' so that the emotional force of the experience—the thing that matters most to the people themselves—was edited out" (Sayer, 2011, p. 3). The everyday practice of mobilities, when treated as a rational thing, comes to be only about time and money. The emotional forces of experiences on the move, how to connect everyday life so that needs are met as much as possible, the freedom, the flexibility, the communities, the activities, are about emotions. Nobody wants to just go from A to B, there is a reason to move and there is a reason to arrive. It is what comes before and after (and don't forget the time spent moving) that matters to people. By discharging emotions, possibilities for change are not revealed, and having as little influence on this process as the potato had on its spread in Western Europe is what remains. Paying attention to emotions is not the same as saying that rationalities or systemic thinking are not important: institutional material arrangements have a significant influence on everyday mobilities but they cannot act in isolation, they must be combined with a consideration of emotions. Sayer underlines this when saying: "I have no truck with a romanticism that attempts to deflate reason or rationality. Rather I argue that, properly understood, reason is involved with all these things" (Sayer, 2011, p. 4). Taking emotions seriously does not equal romanticism, it means taking seriously what actually prompts practices.

When livable cities (currently a very significant issue in the international competition between cities) are presented, the visualizations and arguments are based on emotions. To validate the competition, a variety of measuring tools are used for comparing cities: "...livability must be understood not as a singular quantifiable aspect of urban space, but rather as a way in which (local) governments relate to their territories and their inhabitants" (Johansen, 2021, p. 45). No matter how rationally and measurably the livable city is presented, it is the emotions, the happiness, the freedom that are center stage. And this is most frequently without cars, at least in the visualization. The livable city is, as Johansen (2021) discusses, a strategy for urban planners but is at the same time also comparable to utopias or other futurist imaginations, primarily focusing on positive emotions and the good life. This is in opposition to the way the city, its everyday life, and its mobilities are often described in predictions about automation as the new promising sustainable technology.

Looking through the movies or images produced by using automation as a search term on Google brings you to descriptions of clean environments where different automated technologies are sliding effortlessly through the city, a city that, except for its buildings and corridors, looks very little like the one we see when we step out of the door. The idea presented is also that a new flexibility and freedom will emerge. Suddenly, the physical movement becomes a place for working, sleeping, or partying. My favorite example is a picture of an automated car with a dog and a teenage girl (occupied with looking at her phone) in the front seats. In the back seat is a two-year-old (in a child seat, of course) smiling happily. The story this photo wants to tell is one of freedom and flexibility. Parents no longer need to think about shuttling kids back and forth to day care or school, the automated car takes care of this trivial everyday routine. The major problem here is the assumption that parents of the future no longer have a need to make sure that their small child is arriving in day care and being met by that other responsible adult that they trust to take care of their child. The everyday routines, might be trivial, but also most often infused with love, compassion, and caretaking.

Another favorite visualization is a film clip where Arthur C. Clarke (author of the book *2001: A Space Odyssey*) predicts the internet in

1964. Here he describes quite precisely how virtual mobilities will look in the future. The idea that it would be possible to talk to people on the other side of the globe and that people could conduct their business from Haiti or Bali even if the office were in London was quite radical and unimaginable in the 1960s. Where he was quite wrong in his predictions, however, was that the virtual mobilities would make physical mobilities come to a halt. His prediction that the city as a meeting place for individuals would cease to exist also does not mirror the present. The path he followed, together with many others, was that technologies would replace the emotional need that physical meetings fulfil. Castelles points out this misunderstanding in the new introduction to the second edition of *The Rise of the Network Society*:

> ...the predictions of futurologists over the last 20 years have not come to pass. The death of the city has been announced a thousand times, for example. The reasoning behind this declaration was that the modern communication technologies and the internet would render the city redundant, as individuals could remain connected regardless of where they lived... (Castells, 2010, p. vi)

This does not mean that we should not also believe in technology, and Castells also urges us to take it seriously, but he also emphasizes that we need to keep in mind that "the search for identity is as powerful as techno-economic change" (Castells, 2010, p. 4). It is tempting to believe in technology as the thing that can solve the issues related to climate change, and technology is indeed a powerful assistant in everyday life. It is, however, just one side of the coin: the good city, quality of city life, and the future of the next generation cause other issues to come to the surface. With the current need to change to more sustainable practices in everyday life mobilities, the values of everyday life must be part of the strategy for change. This gives planning the added responsibility of responding to the needs for and aspirations toward the good city, and the question of what kind of city with which mobilities becomes essential. Today's city planning is still influenced by the legacy of Marinetti/Futurism and Le Corbusier, not least in relation to mobilities. They are often presented as extreme examples of misanthropic city planning, but in their time their ideas were utopias aiming at creating a better life in cities. In the following, a utopian starting point for creating better futures will be discussed to emphasize why they are still very much needed.

Utopias as horizons for change

Throughout modern life, there has been a long tradition of creating utopias of real places with an emphasis on the space and the imagined communities inhabiting these places. These utopias had an extensive spatial order where each and every form and function of life was laid out. In these utopias, the dwelling places were the glue that bound together all social relations (Amin and Thrift, 2002; Pinder, 2005). The mobilities connecting these dwelling spaces was based on a rational starting point—focusing on zero friction. It was a time when the technologies of mobilities, especially the car, became a common household item, a liberating technology that entailed the promise of individual life planning. When Ebenezer Howard (1902) wrote *Garden Cities of Tomorrow*, his proposals were seen as a solution to what he saw as the problems created by big cities stemming from unhealthy living conditions and pollution from production. In his utopia, Howard was very focused on rethinking the institutional material arrangements and their concrete problems. The Garden City was about clean air to breathe, green spaces, and institutions and facilities that could accommodate healthier living and working. Through rational and efficient localization, communication, and transport, the Garden City was seen as attracting factories and merchants and resulting in skilled workers residing in balanced, socially diverse neighborhoods (Tonboe, 1993). Howard's Garden City is a good example of how the various aims and ideas embodied in these utopias encountered unexpected consequences once the attempt was made to put them into practice Howard wanted to build "New Towns" as independent "finished" towns of limited size, close to the city. What it was impossible to know at that time was that the penetration of the family car would mean that the Garden City and "New Towns" planning would result in suburbs and a subsequent urban sprawl (Freudendal-Pedersen and Kesselring, 2018b). Howard's Garden City and Le Corbusier's Radiant City were utopias that aimed at creating better living conditions in the dirty and unhealthy cities of their time, but instead they ended up inspiring a functionalistic planning paradigm still prevalent today, a planning paradigm where the lived everyday life with all its emotions is not very present.

These unintended consequences for some became visible quite early on and were heavily criticized. In her book *The Life and Death of Great American Cities*, Jane Jacobs saw the utopia as one erasing communities:

> Le Corbusier's Utopia was a condition of what he called maximum individual liberty, by which he seem to have meant not liberty to

do anything much, but liberty from ordinary responsibility. In his Radiant City nobody, presumably, was going to have to be his brother's keeper any more. Nobody was going to have to struggle with plans of his own. Nobody was going to be tied down. (Jacobs, 1961, p. 22)

The criticism that the utopias of the 1960s became a project of individualization is also what Bauman (2005) emphasizes in his book *Liquid Life*:

Drawing the maps of utopia that accompanied the birth of the modern era came easily to those who drafted them: they were just filling in the blank spots or repainting the ugly parts in the grid of public space whose presence was, and with good reason, taken for granted and seen as unproblematic. Utopias, images of the good life, were matter-of-factly social since the meaning of the 'social' was never in doubt – it was not yet the 'essentially contested issue' it was to become in our day, in the aftermath of the neoliberal coup d'état (Bauman, 2005, pp. 151–152).

The 1960s was a time when the ongoing modernization of societies and technological development sparked the imagining of futuristic cities. These utopias often had futuristic transport systems based on monolithic megastructures. The Archigram group and Cedric Price, with their playful ideas, were two of the influential players at this time, pushing the frontiers of what a city and its mobilities could be. Their focus was on emphasizing humanity and the lived life. However, another strong voice came from Futurism, the Italian art movement founded by Marinetti, with the goal of celebrating the modern area and its technologies. Marinetti created a "Manifesto of Futurism" in 1909 in which he celebrated the beauty of speed, followed in 1947 by Le Corbusier with his Radiant City (Jensen and Freudendal-Pedersen, 2012). Modern planning in particular picked up on ideas from Marinetti and Le Corbusier but their different and imaginative utopias of the perfect city ended up producing multiple problems. For a while at the end of the twentieth century, this led to the idea of utopias being discarded. According to Amin and Thrift (2002), this was partly because the number of possible utopias multiplied but also because new technologies were eroding the imaginative pulse that could create new utopias. These technologies meant that utopian social relations become a "…mass mimesis which adjusts what people feel themselves to be: an exercise in self-construction thereby becomes an exercise in self-expression" (Amin and Thrift, 2002, p. 116).

The publication of David Harvey's *Spaces of Hope* (2000) was a decisive step toward reintroducing utopias in social sciences. What marked the big difference was the focus on utopias of processes instead of spatial forms His focus was on "a spatiotemporal utopianism—a dialectical utopianism—that is rooted in our present possibilities at the same time as it points towards different trajectories for human uneven geographical developments" (Harvey, 2000, p. 196). In the book, Harvey is aware that the utopias of social processes may also have unintended consequences, but he argues that choices have to be made and utopias need spatial form. It is a reaction to the "both/and" that individualizing modernity imposed with too much freedom and the ambivalences that arise as a result of this. Instead, he argues that we need to close some paths and open others, we need to decide for an "either/or," and handle the consequences from these decisions when they arrive. The argument is that when there are no utopias, when there are no visons of how the future might look, the consequence is a reproduction of the unequal and unsustainable society modernity produced. Without a utopia, fighting for a different or better world disappears.

David Pinder follows this idea in his book *Visions of the City* (2005). Here he points out how utopias make us realize what it is about the present that we are not happy with, what needs to be changed. He points to a focus on the people inhabiting the city, not only the institutional material arrangements: "A critical utopianism for today should not be afraid of demanding what has been deemed impossible so as to expand possibilities. It should also recognize the centrality of desire in utopian thought and action, the desire for a different and better life" (Pinder, 2005, p. 262). This desire for a better life, the emotions of desire, is what makes possible what Lefebvre calls "possible impossibles." This stands also as an inspiration to Pinder's work. In Ruth Levitas (2013, p. xi) book *Utopia as Method: The imaginary Reconstitution of Society*, she moves the discussion further and argues for utopias as a tool, as a method because:

It provides a critical tool for exposing the limitations the limitations of current policy discourses about economic growth and ecological sustainability. It facilitates genuinely holistic thinking about possible futures, combined with reflexivity, provisionality and democratic engagement with the principles and practices of those futures. And it requires us to think about our conceptions of human needs and human flourishing in those possible futures.

Using utopias as a horizon for change keeps dreams alive, they can visualize the emotions related to belonging to a community with close connections and can create an awareness of and collaboration on change: "We need to imagine just what a clean, safe, efficient, dynamic, stimulating, just city would look like concretely; we need those images to confront critically our masters with what they should be doing – and it is exactly this critical imagination of the city which is weak" (Sennett, 2007, p. 290). Everyday life in the second modernity has different cultures, needs, and values, also affected by variables such as class, gender, education, and location, but the dreams of hopes are very much alike. Community, freedom, safety, and a future for the next generation emerge as important points. Utopias can shake the fragile irrationalities of the organization of everyday life, but a bigger problem is if imaginations, dreams, and utopias disappear, so we don't think beyond the already existing. The following quotation is an example of these considerations from a focus group discussing how the perfect life could look;

- I think it could look very much like the life I have now
- Well, it must be because we are happy I guess
- Yes, or maybe it is because we can't imagine anything apart from the life we are already living.

The last line here sums up quite well the difficulties with practice change. Imagining the routinized everyday life that provides stability in the mobile risk society in a different way is difficult. Utopias can help to open up the possibility of imagining this everyday life in new ways, they can depict a horizon of change that can be a common project aimed at creating new types of communities. A small-scale example is the future workshops. Here the aim is that participants create new visions for the future when they are provided with a space in which to unfold them (Drewes Nielsen, 2006; Nielsen and Nielsen, 2006). The following quotes come from two future workshops held in connection with the *Mobilities Futures and the City* project (Freudendal-Pedersen and Kesselring, 2016; Kesselring and Freudendal-Pedersen, 2021). What is interesting here is how the participants reflect on the experiences of working with utopias: "It was the balance [between the critique, utopian, and realization phase] that made me feel that it had a purpose and I felt quite playful because of the atmosphere. And it is not easy at all to make someone like me play." Another participant, who is familiar with creative methods and who uses them in his own work, stated: "Everything was so light and playful and the distance between you and others disappeared. I have never experienced such methods before. People got very close very quickly, and you couldn't have managed this with other approaches." These quotations show the enjoyment gained from working with utopias but also how perspectives toward other disciplines are broadened. The aim of the two workshops was to think about how future mobilities in cities could look and the invited participants were from industry, planning, architecture, and art. The workshop showed the potential of utopian thinking in urban mobilities planning, a point Freidman also makes: "Utopian thinking, the capacity to imagine a future that is radically different from what we know to be the prevailing order of things, is a way of breaking through the barriers of convention into a sphere of the imagination where many things beyond our everyday experience become possible" (Friedman, 2002, p. 103). With this quotation in mind, we now focus on the role of planning in creating different futures.

The power of stories in planning future mobilities

There are a large number of different ways to approach the question of planning—and the question of what planning theory is has many answers. In his book *Insurgencies: Essays in Planning Theory*, Friedman states that planning theory is "cobbled together from elements that were originally intended for altogether different uses" (2011, p. 131). Planning is a practice, but it is also a certain way of thinking about the future. "Planning is an intervention with an intention to alter the existing course of events" as Fainstein and Defilippis (2016, p. 8) put it in their introduction to the fourth edition of *Readings in Planning Theory*. Recently I decided to catch up and watch Game of Thrones. For those (probably very few) readers who haven't yet seen the most watched series ever, it is full of killing, kings and queens, war, sex, and magical creatures. One of the main characters, a political strategist—in the end of the series when everything is about war, bloodshed and losing and gaining power—says more than once that it is not the bloodline (from the kings and queens) that gives power, it is in the right story that power lies. Telling the right story in the right way so that it gains power is what is essential.

That we tell stories is not a new thing, it has been going on since the birth of humanity and utopias are a way of telling stories. When Forrester and Fisher published *The Argumentative Turn in Policy Analysis and Planning* in 1993, it was a significant step toward understanding the *role* of stories in policy and planning. They start out by asking the question "What if our language does not simply mirror or picture the world but instead profoundly shapes our view of it in the first place?"(Fischer and Forester, 1993, p. 1). When new areas in a city need to be developed, it is very often architects that create the local plan, the visualization of how it can look. With their visualizations they tell the stories used to convince politicians to say "yes" to the local plan, people to agree at citizen meetings (if such are held), and entrepreneurs to build in the areas. Through this narration, the framework for urban areas is created. Visualizations of new urban areas often depict people dwelling in urban green areas. In some cities in particular, the physical mobilities depicted are cycling, walking, and public transport. What seems to happen again and again is that this does not necessarily align with what the finished development area looks like. There is an inherent logic that people with money want to have a car: as new urban developments have very expensive apartments, those buying them will by definition have the necessary resources to buy cars, thus more parking spaces than depicted in the original plan is a must. In reality, this means that the visualizations used to convince policy makers and planners about developing the urban area do not tell the full story but this seems to be taken for granted since subsequent protests about it are rare.

It seems like the idea of sustainable mobilities as that which creates livable cities is quite strong—until it has to be put into practice. Recently, one of the bigger cities in Denmark decided that it wanted to be CO_2 neutral by 2030. The city council vote on the decision was unanimous, right across the political spectrum from left to right. To help in deciding how to bring this about, they invited a task force to give recommendations. As a starting point for the task force's work, the municipality put approximate numbers on different areas that needed to reduce CO_2 outputs. In this plan, they suggested that transportation CO_2 outputs should be reduced by 250,000 million tonnes by 2030. The task force in its final recommendations reduced this to 150,000 million tonnes. This was done because even achieving a reduction of 150,000 tons of CO_2 would mean drastic changes for the physical mobilities in the city. What was very interesting was the way the recommendations from the task force (that the politicians asked for) in relation to transportation (whose emissions the politicians wanted to reduce more than the task force ended up doing) were received in the end. The right wing of the political spectrum was especially unhappy about the limitations in relation to private cars and was ready to withdraw from the agreement. This city has, in line with all other cities in Denmark, experienced a continuous increase in car ownership and kilometers driven. Also in line with other Danish cities, CO_2 emissions from transportation is the only area where there has been no reduction at all.

I cannot help but wonder what the politicians were expecting from the task force, but it is clear that even where a common motivation and agreement exist, the private car is still a hot potato. It also underlines that: "...policy-making is a constant discursive struggle over the criteria of social classification, the boundaries of problem categories, the intersubjective interpretation of common experience, the conceptual framing of problems, and the definitions of ideas that guide the ways people create the shared meanings which motivate them to act" (Fischer and Forester, 1993, pp. 1–2). The negotiations surrounding the aim of achieving carbon neutrality by 2030 in the Danish city mentioned above are an ongoing issue and no final decisions had been made when writing this. However, it has been quite fascinating to follow the discussion on social media. Center stage are exactly the same storylines that we have heard repeatedly for the last 50 years: no cars in the city center means that business life will die; people will leave the city when they can't use their car and the city will die; it is impossible to hold down a job if I cannot commute by car; you cannot rely on the public transport system; and, last but not least, my kids cannot get to school or leisure activities. The structural stories come to life.

The structural story is the everyday banal version of what produces and is reproduced by policymaking and its argumentation. Just as "Policy analysis and planning are practical processes of argumentation" (Fischer and Forester, 1993, p. 2), the structural story is a practical process of argumentation that shapes everyday practices. In *The Argumentative Turn Revisited*, Fischer and Gottweis (2012) reflect on 15 years of research within the argumentative turn and how it has developed. They state that the "...argumentative turn seeks to understand the relationship between the empirical and the normative as they are configured in the processes of policy argumentation" (Fischer and Gottweis, 2012, p. 2). What is central is understanding the making of meaning and how this interrelates with the institutional material arrangements of the lived life. This is also a question of the philosophy of science—understanding planning and policy on all scales needs a conversation between materialities and immaterialities. Fairclough et al. (2002) pick up this question in their article "Critical Realism and Semiosis" where they argue that critical realism will benefit from critical discourse theory to understand the making of meaning. "[C]ritical realism has tended to operate with an insufficiently concrete and complex analysis of semiosis. It has tended to take symbol systems, language, orders of discourse, and so on for granted, thereby excluding central features of the social world from its analysis" (Fairclough et al., 2002, p. 9).

One major reason for this might be the "problem" with normativity, a word that for many years has had negative connotations, not least within social science. Sayer describes it this way:

> Social scientists are taught to adopt and prioritize the positive point of view and, unless they also read philosophy, to suppress normative reasoning. The gradual separation of positive and normative thought that has occurred over the last 200 years in social science has involved not only an attempted (though incomplete) expulsion of values from science, but an expulsion of science or reason from values, so that values appear to be mere primitive, a-rational subjective beliefs, lying beyond the scope of reason. (Sayer, 2005, p. 3)

This expulsion of values from science is also prevalent within planning, and not least within transport planning as transport has been viewed as a purely technical issue. In *The Argumentative Turn Revisited*, Fischer and Gottweis (2012, p. 3) argue that values most definitely apply to transport (as well as to many other areas of planning) and underline how "...traditional approaches—often technocratic—have proven inadequate or have failed." This might have a lot to do with the fact that "In everyday life, the most important questions tend to be normative ones" (Sayer, 2005, p. 3) and if the values, feelings, and emotions of everyday practice are not integrated, planning falls short. The rational economic individual is the one planners and politicians are hoping to deal with; the issue is that the emotional individual is also inhabiting this same body, and many of the decisions that this mixed human has to make are not clear cut and tidy; even when they are presented as such, it is rarely convincing. This is one of the main points in the argumentative turn: it is not clear-cut solutions we are faced with but, most of the time, messy challenges:

> By focusing on argumentation, processes of dialogic exchange, and interpretive analysis, we need to discover how competing policy actors construct contending narratives in order to make sense of and deal with such uncertain, messy challenges (Fischer and Gottweis, 2012, p. 7).

Both the structural stories and storytelling in the argumentative turn are closely related to discourses: "Discourses, as such, provide the material from which argumentation, …can be constructed"(Fischer and Gottweis, 2012, p. 11). Discourses form specific ways to understand the world—or a section of the world—and are not easily changed. However, "In relatively stable societies, agents—often in the form of discourse coalitions—can manage to bring about change in discursive practices, albeit gradually" (Fischer and Gottweis, 2012, p. 12). The discourse is an articulated unit which can be used by both small and large groups of people. Different discourses can lead to the same structural story. The structural story "when you have kids you need a car" can come from a discourse about "the good parent" or a discourse about "real men have their own car."

Mobilities are fundamental in society and everyday life, and with the structural stories it is possible to capture—across different discourses—how practices are formed and from what. The same goes for storytelling in planning where "the specific role of the story is to furnish communication with particular details that provide the material out of which social meaning is created" (Fischer and Gottweis, 2012, p. 13). With the "argumentative turn" in policy analysis (Fischer and Forester, 1993; Fischer and Gottweis, 2012; Healey, 1997), attention is given to discursive patterns and structures in society and their development. This also entails a subject-oriented approach in urban planning which sees sustainability and socially cohesive cities as something much more than "nice-to-have" features. It also highlights how the structural stories on everyday mobilities practice show the way "individuals-in-relations" guide everyday practices by reproducing a "normality" or "taken-for-granted naturalness." You could also call them micro-discourses. With the structural story and storytelling we come to understand the significance of everyday life rhythms, hopes, dreams, and expectations (Fischer and Gottweis, 2012; Freudendal-Pedersen and Kesselring, 2016; Sandercock, 2003). Even if this is not the first thing that pops up when interviewing, showing an interest in an interviewee's everyday life stories opens up many new orientations and unveils the complexities of mobilities practices (Freudendal-Pedersen, 2009; Kaplan and Ross, 1987).

Cities, mobilities, and the human scale

Mobilities and their infrastructural systems have been at the center of city planning for the last 100 years. As the above highlights, the cities we have are also dependent on which research approach has been used to understand and shape them. Today, the globalization and cosmopolitanization of societies continues to be praised, though maybe somewhat less so in pandemic times, and much effort and state money continue to be put into keeping major international infrastructure systems like the airline industry, as well as transnational and transregional surface transport networks, afloat (cf. Hajer, 1999, Jensen and Richardson, 2003; Kesselring, 2009). So, while these systems continue to represent the provision of the mobilities and motility of the mobile risk society in the age of second modernity, the 2020–2021 global pandemic has made the risks this also entails even more clear (Bereitschaft and Scheller, 2020; Freudendal-Pedersen and Kesselring, 2021). But the close connection between the development of infrastructures and economic growth has become a primary objective bypassing most other concerns and this is what we can see from much city planning during the last century. The firmly entrenched discourse that more mobility creates more growth means that city planning has centered on creating infrastructural systems, dominated by an autologic which is the internal growth logic of planning systems and policies, and which primarily focuses on the accessibility and efficiency of the private car (Dennis and Urry, 2009). And today the car has become much more "than just a mode of transport, technical device or artefact, which one can use for the purpose of social actions. The car is an essential part of a modern way of life" (Burkart, 1994, p. 220) [my translation]. This autologic has created a locked-in system whereby attempts to change it create strong resistance in everyday life, business, and politics. As Nigel Thrift puts it: "...a hundred years or so after the birth of automobility, the experience of driving is sinking in to our 'technological unconscious' and producing a phenomenology that we increasingly take for granted but which in fact is historically novel" (Thrift, 2004, p. 41).

Sustainable mobilities entail challenging the dominance of the private car. In doing this, it is essential to be aware what we are up against. It is an ongoing topic within the issue of sustainable cities that providing better public transport for people will make them change transport modes. This aligns with an ontology within the traditional research used for planning traffic and transportation in cities. It is based on a belief that changing people's behavior is a cognitive matter (as discussed in Chapter 2), but as Thrift shows, this is not where the everyday practices of car driving derive from. Another story comes to mind from the earlier example I gave about the Danish city that wanted to be carbon neutral. One of the parties on the right that did not want to place limitations on car use stated that they were only interested in using the carrot, not the stick. They were very clear that achieving carbon neutrality in relation to mobilities should occur because something better was being offered. However, this seems to be exactly what we have been trying to do for the last 50 years, so far with no success. It might be that we need a new approach.

Taking mobilities as the starting point, the search for change has to start in a different place where the culture and everyday life practices are at the core. These two things are mutually dependent and are used most visibly in the creation of utopias where the imagined space is connected with the imagined community and its inhabitants. These utopias often have an extensive spatial order where all forms and functions of life are laid out, and the places are seen as the glue which binds all social relations (Amin and Thrift, 2002; Jensen and Freudendal-Pedersen, 2012; Pinder, 2005). As I mentioned at the beginning of this chapter, there are arguments to be made about the unintended consequences of these utopias, but, whatever these may be, they stand as a picture of a future that people could relate to a place they want to live.

There might be a tendency for the technological aspects of the city to be prioritized over the lived life. Technology is undoubtedly important and can create new visions and openness, but can also mean shrinking, unimaginative thinking as well as path dependency. Jane Jacobs' (1961) ideas about the open city are about creating spaces for lived life by creating an unfinished form that have multiple opportunities for use. Through flexible architecture with open space around it an "unfinished" architecture which can be added to appears. Today, planners have an arsenal of technological tools at their disposal and work within a framework of visual form and social function, but the technologies enabling new experiments are subordinate to a dominant idea of order and control (Sennett, 2007, p. 290). The idea of the human city challenges this with its strong focus on slow time, provided by walking, cycling, and micromobilities. Andreas Dalsgaard's 2012 film *The Human Scale* featuring Jan Gehl focuses on the lived life, how it is rarely consciously reflected upon or dealt with, and is therefore difficult to handle in the planning stage (Lyubomirsky et al., 2005). This lack of "data" had already been emphasized by Jan Gehl, the main focus of Dalsgaard's film, in 1966 (2011 in the English version) in his book *Life Between Buildings*, which addressed the importance of holistic (sustainable) planning for urban life. Through a shift in focus away from individuals as rational economic beings when deciding which mobilities to use in everyday life, perspectives on the emotionally driven practice of everyday life mobilities become visible. This can help planning to create a storytelling that responds to the needs and aspirations of citizens and politicians when suggesting alternative mobilities futures in the city (see for instance Freudendal-Pedersen and Kesselring, 2016).

Planning within the mobilities has to deal with the complexities arising from the fact that the traditional definitions of mobility as transport do not help anymore. "Governing without government" (the title of Rhodes' 1996 book), in particular on the local and regional scale, means that the interdisciplinarity of the actors involved in decision-making processes and the diversity of related topics and interdependent fields constantly increases. In particular, large-scale and long-term projects such as train stations, airports, and motorways, but also housing projects, new hospitals, and the spread of IT infrastructures, reveal that the modern planning paradigm, grounded in the rationality that transport problems need to be solved by transport experts and health problems by health experts, is perpetuating problems instead of solving them. Modern planning concepts are guided by the idea that it is possible to develop better planning and make better decisions *FOR* society when a perfect allocation of knowledge and expertise can be secured. Using emotions and utopias is an approach to planning and rethinking mobility *IN* and *WITH* society. Through this approach, a significant potential for an alternative approach toward planning the future of urban mobilities emerges. Instead of relying on even more complex models and simulations, the way forward could be setting up an interdisciplinary social structure where storytelling (Sandercock, 2003) and the genesis of a new argumentative rationality and construction of desirable mobilities futures are possible. Taking articulation and storytelling as our starting point enhances what Hajer (2017) calls "ontological expansion," the transformative capacity of planners to create things that don't exist, to use the imagination and emotions to develop futures that people want to participate in.

6 Futures

Everyday life and its inherent emotions need communities where recognition and approval of belonging is essential. In the age of individualization, there was a tendency for communities to be taken for granted and their importance was underestimated. The opportunities for individual freedom and design of life politics created a tension between individuality and community, security and insecurity, freedom and unfreedom as poles creating a continuum, as continuum individuals moves in-between while moving from situation to situation (Eriksen, 2004). Freedom and its close relationship with capitalism, or, more precisely, capitalism and its inherent message of freedom, formed the expectations of the everyday. Creating a sense of security in a world that can be perceived as very insecure was the major goal. Thomas Hylland Eriksen formulates it like this in his (2004, pp. 138–139) book *Røtter og Føtter* (Roots and Feet): "The world is fragmented, but the individuals living on this planet seek connection. The world is unsafe, but most gravitate toward security when they can. The world is becoming more globalized but this does not necessarily lead to its inhabitants becoming more global" [own translation]. The continuous need to find security, to find a place from where to act in relation to the world risk society is what this last chapter will focus on. *Making Mobilities Matter* is about taking individuals and their everyday lives seriously. It is not finding ways for individuals to act but for *individuals-in-relations* to act together in common projects. Here, researchers and planners have a responsibility to help figure out what these platforms should look like and what tools can be used.

To go back to Lefebvre, his starting point was philosophy, which he characterized as the critical conscience in the real world, and he had political optimism as a driving force. Lefebvre criticized planning and policy for dividing the city into distinct functions inappropriate for a lived life. This functionalistic planning paradigm created the dominance of automobility that is today so taken for granted that it becomes part

DOI: 10.4324/9781003100515-6

of what Thrift (2004) calls our "technological unconscious." Lefebvre refers to this as ideological blind spots which survive unnoticed, dominating and destroying the lived life. "Blindness consists in the fact that we cannot see the shape of the urban, the vectors and tensions inherent in this field, its logic and dialectical movement, its immanent demands" (Lefebvre, 2003, p. 40). In Harvey's book *Spaces of Hope* (2000), he focuses on the vectors and tensions global capitalism imposes on the urban. He also sees utopian thoughts as crucial and underlines the fact that it needs a concrete institutional material arrangement and cannot only exist "...as a pure signifier of hope destined never to acquire a material referent" because without the concrete material utopia "...there is no way to define that port to which we might want to sail" (Harvey, 2000, p. 189). Harvey talks about "utopias of spatial form" (e.g., garden cities) and "utopias of social process" (e.g., the free market) as having formed the urban as we know it today. In order to change this, Pinder (2005) points to utopian thought as a stimulus for imagining change and Levitas (2013) suggests using utopia as a method. Urban planning plays an important role here. In his book *Planning in the Public Domain* Friedmann (1987) argues that at this time there was a crisis in traditional forms of planning, when it was first pointed out that: "The widely held belief that planning is anything other than politically charged is an illusion" (Friedmann, 1987, p. 1). In his later work *The Prospect of Cities* (2002), he argues that utopian thinking has two moments; critique and constructive vision. In Chapter 5, I discussed how often in utopian thinking the issue of mobilities is at best opaque and futuristic and at worst not present at all. Where mobilities is in focus, the current technological unconsciousness keeps automobility "locked in" to certain ways of designing, organizing, and practicing (Dennis and Urry, 2009). This and the fact that: "... the everyday rhythms of domestic life have rarely counted as part of the urban, as though the city stopped at the doorstep of the home. But domestic life is now woven routinely into the 'public realm'" (Amin and Thrift, 2002, p. 18) and this means broadening the view of sustainable urban mobilities. In this chapter, I will gather together some of the main points from the book to indicate possible approaches to futuring sustainable urban mobilities.

Seeing the world in a specific way shapes the world accordingly

Recently, I was approached by a journalist who asked me if I wanted to comment on "new knowledge", as he called it, about the values people assign to car ownership and how half of it was not assigned to use value. Basically, the article he referred to was about the freedom, status, and autonomy the car offers. There are two important points here: first, this is not new knowledge but has been extensively researched during recent decades; second, it was knowledge based on a quantitative approach from a technical university modeling the use value. What we can learn from this story is again two things. First, the journalist on several occasions interviewed me on related issues. In these interviews, we also talked about how the car is much more than a mode of transport and the other reason to why it is so important in people's life. The conversations between him and me clearly did not make the same impact as the modeled results did. Second, it seems there is movement in what aspects can be included in modeling transportation, implying a change of the technological unconsciousness the car has inhabited for so many years. The suggestion here is not that all research on sustainable urban mobilities needs to be quantitative and presented as numbers. This research would not have been possible without the decades of qualitative research into the significance of the car. What it does emphasize is the need to move beyond the soft and hard typologies, as discussed in Chapter 2. By keeping this framework, situations like the above appear: one of the main messages of *Making Mobilities Matter* is about breaking out of this straitjacket.

The above example emphasizes values and emotions and it has penetrated the media consciousness because there is a "specific moment," as Lefebvre would call it. The issue of the large and growing level of CO_2 emissions related to car driving cannot be ignored on an agenda containing national and international goals of 70% emission reductions by 2030. Restrictions on driving cars are still (even with the increasing number of cities that have implemented it successfully) unthinkable for many politicians and transport planners. An agenda that is more acceptable is creating urban spaces where living, moving, and dwelling are in the center. In these plans, it is inherently understood that creating livable green cities entails a focus on active green mobilities (the health agenda) and an openness toward the potential of differenced mobilities. These utopian reflections carry the potential to break through the barriers of convention and create common future stories about the quality of the urban (Friedman, 2002; Harvey, 2000; Lefebvre, 1976). This is a way of avoiding painful discussions and focusing on the possibilities or what Braidotti (2019) names affirmative politics. Attempts to change private car use have so far focused for the main part on the carrot methodology, encouraging people to change practice by offering different opportunities. That this has been ineffective is not because of egoism or a lack of ethics or common responsibility. "Paralysis by choice" has become an increasing problem in a world where information saturates our everyday lives, especially when it comes to information about environmental crises. Planning with a focus on the lived life can establish new types of communi ties that can handle local/global responsibilities and transform them into positive futuristic ideas for cities and regions. Mobilities research plays a central role here through its ability to investigate and understand how new types of communities are part of mobile lives that can be transformed into positive future utopias.

Virtual mobilities have made it possible to connect to people, ideas, and communities on a global scale. The opportunities can be used to present individual lifestyles and life politics (Giddens, 1991) and are ordered in different global communities (Facebook, for instance). Individuals belonging to the millennium generation in particular live a life on many virtual platforms: sitting on their own, in their room at their computer, or in a public space on their smartphones. They frequently visit the same places and in doing so become part of the same communities, while at the same time causing trends and ideas to move globally. As mentioned earlier in Chapter 1, Jeremy Rifkin (2014) highlighted how the importance of the car appears to have significantly diminished among millennials. Whereas before acquiring a car and a driving license was a key rite of passage into adulthood, now virtual platforms constitute an equally valid form of transition to explore the world outside the home. This is not unproblematic as there is extensive research highlighting the challenges and dangers associated with virtual platforms and how they can affect children and their caretakers, and this is an issue that needs constant attention. Looking at this through the lens of sustainable urban mobilities, however, creates a shift where access becomes a key component. Music, films, knowledge, and many other resources are shared, and the same applies to many micro-mobilities (such as scooters and e-bikes). The moment that needs to be sized is when the car becomes a mobilities option.

Access versus ownership

Visions of future mobilities are connected to Mobility as a Service (MaaS) and an understanding of mobilities as *accessed* instead of *owned* (Canzler and Knie, 2016). The idea is out there and present in many urban plans but "neotechnological automobilization" is still a dominant response to energy use issues in the shape of automation and e-cars. As Nixon (2012, p. 1673) puts it: "transport decision makers predominantly drive," and "the neotechnological approach allows capture of the consumers' surplus and is less likely to disrupt capital accumulation" (Nixon, 2012, p. 1664). This challenges sustainable urban visions and locks in the myth of "prosperity through mobility" (Essebo and Baeten, 2012), thereby maintaining the car's dominant role. Today, we have a range of services never before seen: car-sharing services like Uber, Lyft and BlaBlaCar, free-floating services like DriveNow and Car2Go, and station-based services. Sharing systems are a growing part of urban mobilities: Uber (recently estimated to be worth close to 70 billion USD) is a major player together with, for instance, Google, Tesla, Alibaba, and Baidu on the global market (Tyfield, 2018). This is not necessarily part of an intended, foreseen, or actively sought strategy but a development brought about by, among other things, the opportunities of virtual mobilities. Multinational car companies like General Motors, Daimler, and Toyota are also reacting to these social transitions in the "system of automobility" (Urry, 2004) and developing new business models that also embrace the car as a shared technology.

Sharing is not a new invention but has always been a part of organizing the everyday. Throughout history, sharing resources, tools, and knowledge has been key to survival and development (Fisher, 1979; Fjalland, 2019; Shiva, 2016). Prior to early capitalism, sharing was primarily concentrated around exchanges of food and other materials, and common ownership of means of mobilities (such as horses and boats). With the advent of capitalism, this expanded to include trading, renting, and leasing and more recently today's buzzwords of "co-creating" and "co-financing." Apart from this, many things that we hardly think about and take for granted are also shared, be it public transport, public libraries, or urban public places. As the mediator, virtual mobilities expanded, or maybe reintroduced, sharing as part of everyday life and business and it is today essential in relation to materials, resources, data, and capital for urban and rural cities and regions (Freudendal-Pedersen and Kesselring, 2018b; Graham and Marvin, 2002; Kesselring et al., 2020; Sheller and Urry, 2006).

The sharing economy concept has been criticized for its paradoxical nature of being "monolithic capitalism" (Tsing, 2009) building on for-profit platforms (Schor and Attwood-Charles, 2017) but within which non-commercial sharing practices are also blooming (Fjalland, 2018; Picard and Buchberger, 2013). The sharing economy is diverse and has both for-profit and non-profit players (Richardson, 2015) but is most often based on an idea of making under-utilized assets accessible with a consequent reduced need for ownership (Stephany, 2015).

Accessibility is the major reason for people to engage in sharing practices related to cars, bikes, food, houses, and, not least, expertise. In this way, what a decade ago was a radical vision is today a part of the norms and values for both institutions and individuals (Mason, 2016; Ostrom, 2012). Even global car producers in some cases become drivers of the sharing economy when they see this as their opportunity to keep market share. This engagement is propelled by increasing attention from global, national, and local governments to CO_2 reduction and the ensuing discussions related to congestion charging, road pricing, and other restrictions on automobility (Freudendal-Pedersen et al., 2016).

An "unintended" consequence of the system of sharing mobilities could be accessibility based more on equality and social participation and increased availability for a wider range of social groups. Large inequalities currently exist in terms of who suffers the unintended consequences of automobility. Low-income urban areas are generally closer to large roads and have fewer opportunities for sharing systems of mobilities. A research project I am currently working on has two neighborhoods in Copenhagen as empirical cases. The wealthy, newly developed urban area has a vast variety of sharing mobilities (including several public transport connections). It is placed by the waterfront with large outdoor public spaces and boasts the most expensive apartments in Denmark and underground parking spaces. The other area is dominated by non-profit housing, is surrounded by three main arterial roads, and has fewer options for public transport. Given the presence of surface parking and expectations of low use, sharing mobilities providers are not interested in the area.

This inequality, created by the current car-centered system, cannot be solved with sharing systems alone, but if sharing is accompanied by restrictions on privately owned cars, access to people, goods, ideas, and services becomes the starting point for city development. A renewed focus on equal accessibility as well as equality in exposure to pollution can have positive affects for integrating MaaS in transport and planning policy (Sheller, 2018). The digitalization of the automotive industry has had a large impact (Fraedrich and Lenz, 2014) and with "automated as shared" becoming part of the future vision of the individual, freedom and self-actualization are being challenged. It seems the global car companies are to the forefront in realizing that if the equation "freedom equals individualized" is no longer automatically accepted, privately owned cars will no longer dominate in an age of climate change the way they did throughout the twentieth century.

A relevant issue is the role of sharing mobilities in the pursuit of big business, as the next phase of capitalist development. As Harvey (2001) points out, capital needs a fixed materiality to expand from and, as with Uber for example, the people themselves shoulder the entire responsibility for and cost of raw materials and labor. They commodify and take the risks while others profit. In this sense, it can be argued that sharing mobilities provides a spatial fix that assists in overcoming new barriers for capital accumulation in urban mobilities (Spinney, 2016). This is also the case with many bike- and scooter-sharing systems where the main incentive is the accumulation of data that can be economically utilized (Spinney, 2020). This gathering of data has created a resource that has so far not been used for the achieving of civic goals. Even if some of the data is open access, it is impossible for users without highly qualified technical skills to utilize this knowledge, making black-boxed datafication a key issue.

Based on this, it seems obvious that the concept of sharing is being utilized by mainstream economics in the search for profit (Martin, 2015; Viba, 2014). In response, a discussion about the difference between sharing and the sharing economy has arisen (Light and Miskelly, 2015). While sharing can be a platform for economic exchange, altruistic community-based cultures of sharing are also part of the picture. Sharing mobilities is therefore not a clear-cut issue and entails the paradox between being *part* of the capitalist economy or providing an *alternative* to the capitalist economy (Kesselring et al., 2020). What is clear cut though is that the sharing of mobilities and MaaS systems are essential for sustainable urban mobilities futures, not only in relation to CO_2 emissions and pollution but just as importantly for the use of space.

Urban mobilities futures

Given a technocratic starting point in approaches to urban transport planning, the issue of space is seldom addressed critically. Recently, a Danish comparison was made between space use in relation to building light rail and building roads. The outcome was that, based on the number of passengers transported at a frequency of six times an hour, light rail was more space consuming than cars and as such nor recommendable for middle sized cities. The resources associated with parking all these cars that were transporting people to the inner city were omitted from the picture. The calculation was based on the premise of the existing status quo: that limiting access for cars is still unimaginable for many researchers, planners, and politicians. If the calculation instead had included the option of only providing two lanes for cars (one in each direction instead of two) and using this extra space for cyclists, pedestrians, and micro-mobilities, then there might be a need for more frequent trips for the light rail and less access for cars and a different picture would emerge. As already mentioned the car is an integral part of many everyday lives and the maintenance and reproduction of its status is based on economic rationalities and its everyday emotional and embodied significance. In his book *The Politics of the Pantry*, Michael Mikulak addresses this dilemma in relation to food and climate change:

> ... what I believe is crucial for addressing the environmental crisis and adapting to climate change, is a profound shift away from this form of top-down, technocratic, disembodied form of knowledge. We need forms of tactile, somatic, situated knowledge that are sensitive to local conditions, individual desires and communities, and which can encourage people to shift toward a different model of pleasure, value, and ethics that can account for nature outside the narrow terms of the economy (Mikulak, 2013, p. 76)

This tactile, somatic, and situated knowledge that Mikulak is calling for is also highly relevant in relation to sustainable mobilities. Implementing MaaS as the main source for physical mobilities is not about offering carrots in the shape of new public transport opportunities or more cycle lanes. It needs carrots together with a stick: not until car use is much more restricted will we see a radical change in everyday mobilities. Implementing restrictions on cars has so far turned out to be a difficult political decision. What has, on the other hand, been quite successful is redesigning urban agglomerations with more focus on the allocation of streetscapes for cars, buses, cyclists, and pedestrians. The selling point for this agenda is not climate change but is focused much more on city life.

This agenda has very much been promoted through "tactical urbanism," a phrase coined by Mike Lydon and Anthony Garcia in their book (2015) *Tactical Urbanism: Short-term Actions for Long-Term Change.* What is important here is that the redevelopment of urban space is framed as test scenarios that can inform long-term implementations. This strategy was why it was possible to redesign one of Copenhagen's main neighborhood streets, Nørrebrogade. This street, which connects the inner city with a former working class neighborhood, became gentrified during the 1970s and 1980s, but today has the most ethnically mixed population in Copenhagen, big and small apartments, green areas, and many cafés and bars. When the traffic experiment was decided upon, Nørrebro had 72,000 inhabitants and the highest housing density in the country (Gehl Architects, 2005), with approximately 16,000 cars, 30,000 cyclists, and 26,500 bus passengers using the street on a daily basis (City of Copenhagen, 2013). To address the issue of the lack of space, the City of Copenhagen designed a "Nørrebrogade Program" as a basis for the traffic experiment with three guidelines: (1) The urban space had to be beautified and urban life strengthened. (2) Cyclists' conditions had to be improved on stressed routes. (3) Public transport needed to be strengthened by shortening travel time and making buses more regular (Copenhagen Municipality, 2006). What is interesting here is that cars were not mentioned whereas before the traffic experiment, it was the mobility with the most allocated space. There was a lot of tension when the experiment started but after the trial phase ended the changes were made permanent. The benefits from the redesign meant that Borgerrepræsentationen (the citizen representation in Copenhagen) in 2012 decided to use this approach to redesign other neighborhood streets in Copenhagen (for more details, see Freudendal-Pedersen, 2020).

An important part of the first experiment on Nørrebrogade was the use of prototyping, which is a fundamental part of design methods but has only become dominant in urban planning over the last decade. The main idea is to test things—products or services—as they are developed, concurrently challenging their functionality and reason for being. Through the history of design, prototyping has developed from a simple test of whether the screw fitted the thread into a creative and holistic method to not just test but also develop ideas and proposals. The prototyping of complex product-service systems, experience-based services, and spatial change can take many shapes. In the case of Nørrebrogade, the focus was on colors on the road marking new usage, flower pots and benches, and other dwelling artifacts. As Tom Kelley and Jonathan Littman put it their book *The Art of Innovation*, which later led to the coining of the term "design thinking": "Prototyping doesn't just solve straightforward problems. Call it serendipity or even luck, but once you start drawing or making things, you open up new possibilities of discovery" (Kelly, 2001, pp. 108–109). With prototyping, it is possible to rapidly make tangible what at a given time may seem purely abstract and thereby enable a comprehension of the change in its context and complexity. Prototyping can help open up the potential of utopias and, as Lefebvre put it, can make possible tomorrow what seems impossible today. Prototyping in the context of spatial change is also a way of designing *with* people instead of *for* people. What the Provo group in Amsterdam did with the white bicycles can also be understood as prototyping. It made it possible to localize and analyze (con)temporary physical interventions in the urban space and fabric and ask if and how these functions to change mobilities practices.

Nørrebrogade is just one small example but the concept of tactical urbanism is used in many places, and common to all the experiments is that the main focus is about redistributing space; cars are usually restricted, and active green mobility and meeting and dwelling spaces are put in place. The concept of tactical urbanism also embodies the idea of an emphasis on citizen engagement and ownership. Lydon and Garcia (2015) point out that it is the renewed love affair with the city that to a large degree makes this possible, and starting at the street or block level is the best way forward. This is definitely the way forward where the city administration and politicians are not positively disposed toward any restrictions on automobility.

However, examples of larger plans can also be seen: Ghent's 2017 Circulation Plan was designed to discourage through traffic and make the car less suitable for shorter trips, while Barcelona's superblocks as traffic-regulated cells meant inner streets were mainly reserved for pedestrians and cyclists. In Ghent the focus was on (re)creating the lived city, whereas in Barcelona the main driver was climate change mitigation (Martin, 2021a). Barcelona stands as an excellent example of what Lefebvre would call "a moment." Climate change with heavy rain and the heating of urban areas due to all the asphalt resulted in temperatures in Barcelona up to eight degrees higher than in surrounding urban areas (Moreno-garcia, 1994). This heating up and the flooding from massive rainfalls is much more easily recognizable than CO_2 or any of the other forms of pollution arising from automobility. It is visible and embodied, and recognizing that something must be done and engaging residents becomes easier.

In Robert Martin's 2021 PhD thesis *Points of Exchange – Spatial Strategies for the Transition Towards Sustainable Urban Mobilities*, he uses as inspiration, among other cities, Ghent and Barcelona as a starting point to come up with a plan to redesign Copenhagen. The starting point is a car-free city, not car free as in a life completely without cars, but as a focus on making possible everyday life organization without being car dependent (Martin, 2021a). As an architect, Martin began with the use of visualization to discuss the plan with important stakeholders in two workshops on the development of Copenhagen. The first workshop had a visualized suggestion for how this might be designed, while the second workshop developed the visualization further based on the discussions in the first workshop. What was most striking about these workshops was that in the first workshop, a frequent comment was that it was important not be too radical in developing such a plan for it to be implemented. When returning to the second workshop with developed and detailed visualizations, the general consensus was that it was not radical enough. Martin concludes that "the visualised ideas of the participants became vessels for socio-technical imaginaries" (Martin, 2021b, p. 229) and as such opened up what Hajer (2017) calls "ontological expansion" in relation to the use of storytelling. In other words, utopias for future sustainable mobilities need good stories but also need visualizations to feed the imagination of the urban in a different form from what we already know.

Transdisciplinarity and visualizations

Architects and designers often adopt a clear normative approach to how futures could and should look. This normativity has been eradicated from social science during the last 100 years (Sayer, 2005) but is slowly re-entering, it being essential in order to create possible futures (Davis, 2010). It is imperative here to engage with those mastering the design and visualization professionally. Mobilities researchers can, with their knowledge, critically question the path dependencies, structural stories, and societal discourses addressed or reproduced in the visualizations, but, in most cases, cannot actually produce these visualizations themselves. The ongoing development of mobile methods can be used in order to understand the change from a social science perspective. Mobilities research is transdisciplinary, and when at its best, it bridges disciplines in a Mode 2 science context. Mode 2 science is context-sensitive and understands science and society as co-mingling overlapping arenas (Kemp and Martens, 2007; Nowotny et al., 2001). In the same way, mobile methods can be characterized as Mode 2 methods. Building bridges between the bodies of knowledge that different disciplines take for granted about which methods to use gives completely new perspectives of and understandings about how mobilities are transforming the world—on all scales (Büscher et al., 2020).

As a result of this, new ethical questions emerge. Filming and taking photos stimulate new discussions about privacy issues when moving around with respondents in public spaces. Research on new kinds of online communities or following business travelers' time use and virtual encounters while on the move results in discussions about privacy in relation to virtual communication—is following people online the same as reading their private mail for example? Such issues force mobilities researchers to be clear and reflexive about a whole new series of questions concerning the ethics of research. This refers back to discussions on ethics and responsibilities: is there an epistemological difference between ethics and responsibility or is it ontological? In line with Sayer (2005, p. 146), I would argue that "Lay ethical practices... are concrete and governed by practical reason as well as by rules; it is messy, concrete and practical rather than tidy and concise." This often conflicts with the researcher's requirements to present practices as tidy and concise in order to create resonance and understanding in a wider audience, while also knowing that the start of most things is messy, concrete, and practical (Freudendal-Pedersen et.al, 2014; Freudendal-Pedersen, 2014a).

Here, a focal point is the essential reflexivity needed when engaging in normative research or visual representation, not least in being aware of the seductive perspective some narratives contain. Visual methods have always been an important tool in the dissemination of urban design projects, plans, and visions, partly to illustrate the structure and layout of the actual proposal for, say, land use or infrastructure, partly to illustrate the spaces and the everyday life that will unfold therein after realization of the project. The weight between these two has shifted in favor of the latter, hence today emotionally related visions of the good life are often in the forefront of the actual descriptions of the project and its projected implications on a larger scale. Visualizing proposals for plans and projects demands that a lot of details are catered for early in the project, making it possible to show context, thereby creating very specific images and narratives. The result is complex, tangible, and normative in the sense that it includes a notion of a situation different from the existing one, which as an underlying basis must be seen as better. The very specific images and narratives make it possible to understand large coherences within the project and its external context, and in return be very specific with a criticism of the project—a criticism that might not be possible were the proposers are less explicit in their dissemination of their project.

In relation to sustainable mobilities futures, there are challenges in creating compelling and holistic visions. Sustainable planning and discussions about this issue frequently begin with dystopian projections about the result of not doing anything. Thus any action different from the existing ones becomes good, but without any certain notion or knowledge about the implied consequences (Hajer and Versteeg, 2019). Visual methods hold the ability to support positive and holistic visions of the good sustainable life, taking into account the changes needed but also offering a compelling image of the advantages. Both within social science and design in the realms of urban planning and academic research, visual methods hold a significant potential. Simultaneously, however, they also represent a risk of not fulfilling academic meticulousness in terms of methodology and philosophy of science. The visual methods embody an inherent and unavoidable aesthetic that social scientists, not engaged in visualization research, often lack the methods and ability to fully understand and analyze. An example of all the small elements often overlooked is given by Martin (2021a) in relation to visualizations of AV (autonomous vehicle) futures. He uses the example of Daimler's visualizations for AV futures in the US compared to those used in the EU. The two images are nearly identical, they are clearly aiming to depict a livable city and contain images of pedestrians and cyclists. Very often when the car industry is depicting futures, the car is alone in an urban space. With these images on AV futures, Daimler is tapping into the agenda of AVs as a pathway to sustainable urban mobilities futures entailing more livability and spaces for dwelling. In Martin's article he shows how:

> The image embeds the landscape development of urbanisation through the inclusion of futuristic high-rise architecture, implying that space is at such a premium that city residents are forced to live in smaller and smaller apartments and nature is confined to the facades of buildings. However, in this densified future, road space has actually increased. Physical road features such as pedestrian crossings, sidewalks, and road markings are removed, expanding the domain of AVs while also granting them complete control over when other modes can use the space. For example, the crossing pedestrian depicted in this future may only safely cross the road when the AV allows it, demonstrating that the sociotechnical imaginary presented here by Daimler is one ruled by AVs (Martin, 2021a, p. 5).

The full dominance of the AV in these visualizations can also be seen in relation to cyclists: bike paths only go around corners but do not cross intersections. It is very likely that most mobilities researchers would pick up on these inequalities reproduced in the visualizations, but it is just as likely that most planners and politicians would overlook them. These images therefore have the ability to seduce the viewer so that they forget to be aware of the implicit inequality that maintains the car in its dominant position.

Working in transdisciplinary environments that include professionals who are experts in visualization is an important way forward when suggesting sustainable urban mobilities futures. With visual methods, new ways of understanding and approaching mobilities and urban planning issues emerge and can counteract the reification and path dependency that are so taken for granted they become invisible. This includes carefully discussing decisions about the selection and deselection process surrounding the choice of pictures, events, and situations, a process that is not clear to the viewer. Architectural visions are often much more focused on solving spatial problems and selling solutions than to solve societal problems. Combining Architectural visions with solid analyses of societal problems and understanding the societal and spatial development that created the current problems and caused them to reproduce can provide the outset for planning for sustainable mobilities.

The main point here is to remember asking the right questions and not only present glossy solutions when it is unclear what the roots of the problems are. The right questions need both an internal and external critique. Important questions to ask are, for instance, if the scenarios and visualizations are expert-driven pictures of their wishes, or are they more democratic and also include lay people's wishes and dreams for their future daily lives? In visualization, as in all other research, the transparency of the research process is what makes it possible for others to understand and assess the quality of the product. Also, in visualizations "thick descriptions" (Kvale and Brinkmann, 2009, p. 67) entailing detailed descriptions on the course of the project, choices in relation to intentions, concepts, critical view, and effects and affects needs to be provided and discussed openly for others to understand the final result. Visualizations are often much shorter and more concise than written research results and this means a very selective representation. However, they also represent an essential entry point into imagining futures, including elements that might seem impossible.

This is especially important when the smartness of cities is increasing. Visualizations of smartness are in many cases presented cleansed of human interactions. It is imposed with an order and cleanliness of the everyday that is not in keeping with the reality of emotional and messy everyday life practices. That the future must be smart is a pervasive discussion in politics, planning, and research, but what does it mean that something is "smart"? And does it equal expensive equipment and new technology? First of all, smart technologies are already embedded in much of the everyday life: traffic signals, train tracks, time-controlled heating, washing machines, ovens, and so forth. This does not, however, mean that smart is automatically good in every situation. Rather it requires researchers, politicians, and planners to critically focus on future everyday lives and determine which problems can best be solved using smart technology.

Smart cities

The excitement surrounding smart cities often becomes grounded in an engineering logic where the promise is an optimization of urban infrastructure and networks and, consciously or not, that also means elements of human interactions (Kitchin, 2015). The idea is that coded spaces can facilitate the efficient use of a city's infrastructure, energy, and spaces. It is thought of as socio-technical environments based around artificial intelligence and IT that will provide user-friendliness and sustainability (Rochet, 2018). It is an idea that views assemblages of technologies as able to increase competitiveness, efficiency, and also social inclusion (Allwinkle and Cruickshank, 2011). This social inclusion is often presented as an opportunity for those who are mobility impaired to be able to move freely, especially through automated technologies. In this way, the promise becomes that smart cities can solve urban problems, as well as those related to climate change, while simultaneously increasing economic prosperity. The issue of citizen participation is handled through innovative technologies, infrastructure, and data management techniques (Hajer, 2016; Hollands, 2014). Thinking about smart cities only from these perspectives is an enforcement of the technocentric planning paradigm where the focus is kept on movement with the single goal of seamlessly moving from A to B as the unchallenged principle underlying the efficient organization of societies (Canzler and Knie, 2016). Smart is good and it holds many opportunities, but it needs to be integrated with the human scale of the city. This means that social and cultural practice needs to be systematically integrated into scientific analysis, planning, business models, and collaborative work on the future of urban living and working conditions.

It seems somehow counter-intuitive to argue against smart cities because "who can be against what is smart – against progress" and this gives the smart city discourse an inherent normative character. So far this has resulted in limited research critically investigating the underlying principles and ideas of the smart city as a model or its spatial, cultural, and socioeconomic implications (Freudendal-Pedersen et al., 2019). This lack in the research has prompted researcher to discuss urban smartness with a focus on the need to include small-scale initiatives, governance, and participation in the processes as essential in the creation of a digitalized urban fabric. Hajer and Pelzer (2018) argues that what we need is smart urbanism rather than smart cities, to design not just expected futures but rather desirable futures. This is in line with the argument presented by Urry in his book *What is the Future* (2016). He begins by asserting that the problems that afflict modern societies need to be analyzed in terms of historical and social conditions and their socio-material and socio-technological environments in order to be able to create desirable futures. For this to happen transdisciplinary and cross-sectoral methodology is essential to create an understanding of all the elements that make cities. Thinking about the technologies that can be implemented in the urban space will not do it alone, it needs to be merged with a strategy of collecting multiple shared perceptions of the aim and culture of future mobilities. Kitchin (2015) also touches upon the ideological nature of the smart cities discourse, especially those arising from its "one-size-fits-all" narrative. Through such rhetoric, the inconsistencies, antagonisms, and conflicts disappear and context loses significance; it is therefore important to "illuminate the ways in which the concept is bound up in the shifting rhetoric and socio-spatial processes of governance and economic development" (Kitchin, 2015, p. 132). This is needed to better understand the appeal smart cities have for stakeholders, making it difficult for them to see alternatives.

With mobilities this means that many stakeholders see "smart" as synonymous with new technological solutions such as automation. However, smart in relation to sustainable mobility can also be to reap the "low-hanging fruit" of already existing innovative mobility-related solutions, which are about creating green and climate-friendly cities where integrated mobility solutions with a central focus on cycling, walking, and public transport. In connection with the EU Jean Monnet Network "Cooperative, Connected and Automated Mobility: EU and Australasian Innovations (CCAMEU)" I arranged a workshop on the "Smart and Liveable City" in Copenhagen. The workshop had participant from the top management in Copenhagen Municipality, Consultancy firms, NGO's and researchers, all people with strong influence on the development of Copenhagen. The most surprising result from the workshop was the consensus that formed around going for the "low hanging fruits." There was no interest in thinking in new smart technologies or technocratic visions. On this day, in this forum, a general agreement was reached that it made more sense to utilize better what was already available in order to move toward more sustainable mobilities. I was surprised and so was my fellow researcher from the network. It was not a dismissal of automation and smartness but a focus on utilizing better what was already available.

This is a smart sustainable mobility culture that is not only about technology, but also how modern life is affected by planning, quality, and structures in the cities we live in. Creating sustainable cities and communities is very much about understanding that mobilities is much more than speed, efficiency, and accessibility. To begin with, the need to create and gather together a comprehensive body of knowledge on materialities for active green mobility using smart data collection systems seems obvious. There is a large amount of data produced for cars in relation to every aspect of their infrastructure, whereas such knowledge in relation to cycling and walking is scarce. The majority of route planners are made for cars; even if there is a cycling option, the data on the small shortcuts, green routes, and similar information is not available. A smart city is a place where a complete inventory of all sidewalks, streets, green routes, cycle paths, and superbike paths would be available. It is a city where data is produced about mobilities experiences, preferences, and desires that can aid in creating future sustainable cities. It is a system that is just and fair in the collection and distribution of data and does not favor specific forms of mobilities. This will make links between all forms of mobilities a prerequisite in developing and accessing a future with access as a key element.

Freedom and rhythms in urban mobilities

The way things look and how they work are inextricably linked (Jacobs, 1961). If good urban spaces are created with space for play, creativity, movement, and relaxation, communities form that want to preserve and maintain these qualities. If the quality of the urban space is not high, why not take the car straight to the front door— it's more convenient. Good urban spaces require peace and security, two qualities not associated with car traffic unless you are sitting inside the car. Spinney (2010) describes how the rhythm of the modern city is subject to the hybrid car driver and how all other types of mobilities become subject to this rhythm. It thus also means that the design of the physical space together with the (un)written rules and symbols try to define how we should move around by making certain types of movements, rhythms, and routes easier to follow than others. According to Spinney, this gives rise to improvised rhythms and routes in the marginalized road users, as they visually assess the properties of the space differently from the facilitation of the dominant order. In Copenhagen, the rationale of the automobile is strong, but in many places, the rhythm of the bicycle is becoming as dominant as that of the car. This is due not least to the cyclists' self-understanding, which is largely supported by the City of Copenhagen's communication strategies (Copenhagen Municipality, 2011, 2019). In many contexts, cyclists perceive "cyclists' space" as an independent rational space, where improvised—or inappropriate—movement patterns and rhythms are more often associated with how the cycling space is designed and attempts to control it. The story of Copenhagen and the Copenhageners is that cycling is regarded as an environmentally sound, time-efficient, and relatively safe mode of transport. This has an impact on how the image of the cyclist generally fits into the narrative of modern everyday life's expectation of lifestyle choices, flexibility, and freedom—among cyclists, non-cyclists, and all those who perceive themselves as somewhere in between.

In the article "Mundane mobilities, banal travels" (Binnie et al., 2007), daily movements in space are described as what "routinizes" our everyday lives, so that reliable rhythms and recognizable repetitions are created. This mundane realm offers conditional possibilities for certainty and security, allowing us to order our everyday life-worlds with a necessary degree of predictability and comfort. Through recognizable, dynamic repetition in everyday life, personal relationships are created with the local, the authentic, the safe, the fixed, and the delimited—which previously, according to Massey (2005), had been linked to the idea of the static place. The place and the context of mobilities thus become the central relationship when individuals seek to create belonging and predictability in everyday life. This familiarity with forms of mobilities also produces an embodied, embedded, and often unreflexive sense of place which is not merely confined to the locations that are joined together by regular journeys but which also exists in the experience of mobility en route. The habitual mobility creates an unreflected sense of the places we move through. The places become familiar and reliable, where the routine enables us to achieve a kind of "linger-in-motion"—a feeling of being in the place, despite the movement through it (Binnie et al., 2007; Spinney, 2007). This is of great importance in relation to the cyclists' sense of flow when they cycle through the city. In movements through places and spaces, individuals must constantly relate and act according to the social and physical relationships that are co-actors in the places. The work with cycling in Copenhagen has shown that this narrative is just as widespread among cyclists—and it is just as important in the choice of everyday mobility. The struggle for urban space is thus also a struggle to maintain the sense of flow that the bicycle sometimes gives. Cyclist in Copenhagen tells stories about the freedom of the bike, sliding through the city, changing direction, whizzing past the queuing cars, and so on. The bicycle was also the first mode of transport that provided the opportunity to move freely and this feeling is maintained and adds to the sense of freedom associated with the bicycle. For some, it even becomes a political statement related to the battle for space and the conflict between motorists and cyclists (Freudendal-Pedersen, 2015b).

This is comparable to the relationship individuals have with the car (Freudendal-Pedersen, 2018) and this provides an insight into the role of mobilities' emotional and embodied relationship with everyday life. By taking seriously how people feel about and in cars, and how they feel that the car culture elicits specific ways of life, we will be in a better position to re-evaluate the ethical dimensions of car consumption and the moral economies of car use: "... Only then can we consider what will really be necessary to make the transition from today's car cultures (and the auto-motive emotions that sustain them) to more socially and environmentally 'responsible' transportation cultures" (Sheller, 2004, p. 224). The fact that both car drivers and cyclists manifest the same emotional parameters, with clear similarities between the emotional elements, is a generally positive thing. The conflicts that arise when envisioning future sustainable mobilities is a struggle to maintain everyday life organization as it is. It clarifies the importance of research, politics, and planning respecting and acknowledging the emotional aspects of everyday life mobilities and that the opportunity to utilize this knowledge in transitions toward sustainable mobilities futures be provided.

Responsibility and opportunities from the unknown

In *Making Mobilities Matter* it is important to integrate that which touches on human emotions and transforms sensitivity to the city, its infrastructure, buildings, and technologies into the planning of institutional material arrangements. Ideas about sustainability can be expressed and made visible through thinking about the relations between humans, infrastructures, products, and buildings. Lefebvre opens up the question of what can be changed, or how we change the world: "...what matters is to grasp movement and non-movement in the present, to grasp what it is that shifts and collides with that which does not shift" (Lefebvre, 1976, p. 14). Moments are defined by a shape and have a constant over time as an element common to a wide range of events, situations, and dialectical moments. *Making Mobilities Matter* is about grasping the moment of a growing acknowledgement that in order to handle climate change, we need to include the human factors as well. In Chapter 4, Communities on the Move, I discussed the significance of sharing responsibility with communities as an important pathway to change. In *Staying with the Trouble,* Haraway points out that:

> We are all responsible to and for shaping conditions for multispecies flourishing in the face of terrible histories, and sometimes joyful histories too, but we are not all response-able in the same ways. The differences matter – in ecologies, economies, species, lives. [...] Many kinds of absence, or threatened absence, must be brought into ongoing response-ability, not in the abstract but in the homely storied cultivated practice (Haraway, 2016, p. 132).

What mobilities has the ability to contribute is not only how to have sustain(ability) but also to have a response(ability) to mobilities' role in relation to climate change. The ability to respond to a common good is, from an everyday life perspective, challenged. This should not be mistaken for egoism, nor lack of ethics. Individuals can feel responsible but without feeling they have the ability to respond. Zeitler (1998) proposes "response-ability" as a keyword in ethical theory as well as in mobility and planning: "Proper responses depend on our ability to respond, our 'response – ability.' This implies that there are limits to our response-ability, both with regard to its extension and with regard to its quality" (Zeitler, 2008, p. 233). Zeitler understands ethics as ontology coming from our sense of right and wrong, our build in normativity. He elaborates on this through a critique of the current traffic system: "...speed is only possible when disregarding the moral circumstances of the actor's social and natural environment. Comfort is achieved only when externalising the 'costs'. Traffic segregation is both detrimental to safety and to the development of our moral judgement" (Zeitler, 2008, p. 238). With the last point Zeitler argues that the segregation of traffic means that we forget to be attentive to others and instead focus on own rights in the traffic system.

Modern everyday lives are characterized by speed, by instantaneous time, the ability to and expectation of constantly and instantaneously reacting to the knowledge and opportunities we get from virtual and physical mobilities. Simultaneously, clock time, imposed by modernization, still plays a vital role in everyday lives. The organization and planning of everyday life with work, school, and leisure activities is organized by clock time. This means navigating and planning an everyday life within clock time, while instantaneous time imposes expectations for the good life that is the goal to achieve. The need to navigate this and constantly commute between these two time-conceptions does not make it appealing to change the everyday mobilities that keep the organization carefully orchestrated in a way that can fulfill one's own and societal expectations. Lived lives have different expressions and opportunities, decided by factors such as class, gender, education, and location. However, emotions, dreams, and the need for ontological security based on wants and desires, security, safety, and communities is something all have in common. *Making Mobilities Matter* is also about shaking the fragile irrationalities holding everyday life together. But, with imagination and utopias, we can create the response-ability to not forget how to play and live lives beyond the existing "frames."

Response-ability is also about understanding other social realities, wishes, and preferences. This respect and open-mindedness are only attained by a clear and conscious approach to one's own ethics own ontology (Freudendal-Pedersen et al., 2014). Being conscious of this impacts the empirical work and creates an understanding that we cannot, through the empirical, access an objective social reality, independent of the researcher. The empirical plays a significant role within mobilities research and has initiated a development within traditional methodological approaches. The mobile methods are described by Büscher and Urry (2009) as providing an opportunity to develop new critical engagements with the future. Response-ability does not make a clear epistemological distinction between ethics and responsibility. As Sayer (2005) points out, lay normativity and morality also entail good heartedness, benevolence, compassion, gratitude, and similar qualities. The paralyzing tendencies of the risk society, making people feel they have no ability to respond or make a difference, need an alternative vision. In Harvey's book *Spaces of Hope*, he asks the question, in the context of Margaret Thatcher's "there is no alternative" slogan in relation to the free market: "how can we have such lack of imagination that we believe there is no alternative?" (Harvey, 2000, pp. 154–156). The human city or, in the context of the global city competition, the livable city, with its irregularities and communal life is not about technological feasibility, based on existing data, models, and calculations. Instead, the questions "why," "for what," and "for whom" are the alternative to the dominating technocratic view on future urban mobilities. This needs transdiciplinarity, not only within the mobilities circles but with other research disciplines, stakeholders and citizens and also as Hajer and Versteeg (2019, p. 10) points to:

> The type of transdisciplinary research needed is one in which we all, as academics, give serious thought to the legitimation of our research orientation and knowledge production – not as an afterthought or in a 'box' of a research application, but as part of the process of the research endeavour.

Making Mobilities Matter is about strengthening the impact of mobilities research. In this book, it is related to in urban planning, but this is equally relevant for other empirical fields. The present focus on climate change, and the changes needed to mitigate the consequences, needs a broader and more inclusive approach in science and practice. With mobilities, perspective changes and new pathways and possibilities to achieving sustainable futures will open up.

References

Aagaard Nielsen, K., Svensson, L.G., 2006. Action Research and Interactive Research: Beyond Practice and Theory. Shaker Publishing B.V, Maastricht.

Adey, P., 2009. Mobility, 1st ed. Routledge, New York.

Adey, P., Bissel, D., Hannam, K., Merriman, P., Sheller, M., 2014. The Routledge Handbook of Mobilities. Routledge, London.

Adey, P., Hannam, K., Sheller, M., Tyfield, D., 2021. Pandemic (im)mobilities. Mobilities. https://doi.org/10.1080/17450101.2021.1872871

Allwinkle, S., Cruickshank, P., 2011. Creating smart-er cities: an overview. Journal of Urban Technology 18, 1–16.

Alvesson, M., Sköldberg, K., 2000. Reflexive Methodology: New Vistas for Qualitative Research. SAGE Publications Ltd, London.

Amin, A., Thrift, N., 2002. Cities: Reimagining the Urban. Polity Press, Cambridge.

Bauman, Z., 2009. Does Ethics Have a Chance in a World of Consumers? (Institute for Human Sciences Vienna Lecture). Harvard University Press, Harvard.

Bauman, Z., 2005. Liquid Life. Cambridge.

Bauman, Z., 2001. Community: Seeking Safety in an Insecure World. Polity, New York.

Bauman, Z., 2000. Liquid Modernity. Polity, Cambridge.

Bauman, Z., 1998. Globalization: The Human Consequences. Columbia University Press, New York.

Bauman, Z., 1995. Life in Fragments: Essays in Postmodern Morality. Blackwell Publishers, Oxford.

Bauman, Z., 1988. Freedom. University of Minnesota Press, Minnesota.

Bech-Jørgensen, B., 1994. Når hver dag bliver hverdag. Akademisk Forlag, Copenhagen.

Beck, U., (2018). Mobility and the cosmopolitan perspective in Freudendal-Pedersen, M., Kesselring, S. (2018) (eds) Exploriing Networked Urban Mobilities. Routledge, New York

Beck, U., 2016. The Metamorphosis of the World. Polity, Cambridge.

Beck, U., 2008. World Risk Society, 2nd ed. Wiley, New York.

Beck, U., 1997. The Reinvention of Politics: Rethinking Modernity in the Global Social Order. Polity, Cambridge.

Beck, U., 1992. Risk Society: Towards a New Modernity. SAGE Publications Ltd, London.

Beck, U., Bonss, W., Lau, C., 2003, The theory of reflexive modernization: problematic, hypotheses and research programme. Theory, Culture & Society 20, 1–33.

Bell, C., Newby, H., 1976. Community, communion, class and community action, in: Herbert, D., Johnson, R. (Eds.), Social Areas in Cities. Wiley, London.

Bereitschaft, B., Scheller, D., 2020. How might the COVID-19 pandemic affect 21st century urban design, planning, and development? Urban Science 4. https://doi.org/10.3390/urbansci4040056

Berger, P.L., Luckmann, T., 1966. The Social Construction of Reality: A Treatise in the Sociology of Knowledge. Anchor, London.

Bergmann, S., Sager, T., 2008. The Ethics of Mobilities (Transport and Society). Ashgate, Franham.

Binnie, J., Edensor, T., Holloway, J., Millington, S., Young, C., 2007. Mundane mobilities, banal travels. Social & Cultural Geography 8, 165–174.

Birtchnell, T., 2016. The missing mobility: friction and freedom in the movement and digitization of cargo. Applied Mobilities 1, 85–101.

Bissell, D., 2019. Transit Life: How commuting is transforming our cities. MIT Press, Cambridge

Bissell, D., 2014. Transforming Commuting. Mobilities: The memory of Practice. Environment. And Planning A: Economy and Space. Vol 46 pp 1946–1965

Braidotti, R., 2019. A theoretical framework for the critical posthumanities. Theory, Culture and Society 36. https://doi.org/10.1177/0263276418771486

Bullard, R.D., Johnson, G.S., 1997. Just Transportation: Dismantling Race and Class Barriers to Mobility, 1st ed. New Society Publishers, Gabriola Island.

Burdett, R., 2010. Endless City. Phaidon Press, London.

Burkart, G., 1994. Individuelle Mobilit{ä}t und soziale integration. Zur Soziologie des Automobilismus. Soziale Welt 2, 216–241.

Büscher, M., Freudendal-Pedersen, M., Kesselring, S., Kristensen, N.G., 2020. Handbook of Research Methods and Applications for Mobilities Research. Elgar, London.

Büscher, M., Urry, J. 2009. Mobile methods and the empirical. European Journal of Social Theory 12, 99–116.

C40 Cities Climate Leadership Group, C40 Knowledge Hub, 2021. 15-minute cities: How to develop people-centred streets and mobility. https://www.c40knowledgehub.org/s/article/15-minute-cities-How-to-develop-people-centred-streets-and-mobility?language=en_US (accessed 7.19.21).

Campisi, T., Basbas, S., Skoufas, A., Akgün, N., Ticali, D., Tesoriere, G., 2020. The impact of covid-19 pandemic on the resilience of sustainable mobility in sicily. Sustainability (Switzerland) 12. https://doi.org/10.3390/su12218829

120 *References*

Canzler, W., Kaufmann, V., Kesselring, S., 2008. Tracing Mobilities – Towards a Cosmopolitan Perspective. Ashgate, Aldershot.

Canzler, W., Knie, A., 2016. Mobility in the age of digital modernity: why the private car is losing its significance, intermodal transport is winning and why digitalisation is the key. Applied Mobilities 1, 56–67.

Cass, N., Faulconbridge, J., 2017. Satisfying everyday mobility. Mobilities 12. https://doi.org/10.1080/17450101.2015.1096083

Castells, M., 2010. The Rise of the Network Society, 2nd ed. Blackwell Publishing, West Sussex.

Castells, M., 1996. The Rise of the Network Society: The Information Age: Economy, Society, and Culture Volume I. Wiley-Blackwell, New York.

Chen, Y., Ardila-Gomez, A., Frame, G., 2017. Achieving energy savings by intelligent transportation systems investments in the context of smart cities. Transportation Research Part D: Transport and Environment 54. https://doi.org/10.1016/j.trd.2017.06.008

Cheng, Y.H., Chen, S.Y., 2015. Perceived accessibility, mobility, and connectivity of public transportation systems. Transportation Research Part A: Policy and Practice 77. https://doi.org/10.1016/j.tra.2015.05.003

Cidell, J., 2012. Flows and pauses in the urban logistics landscape: the municipal regulation of shipping container mobilities. Mobilities 7, 233–245. https://doi.org/10.1080/17450101.2012.654995

City of Copenhagen, 2019. Kommuneplan 2019. Verdensby med ansvar. (Municipal Plan 2019. World City with Responsibility, English Version Late 2020). Copenhagen.

City of Copenhagen, 2013. Evaluation of the Nørrebrogade Project – Stage One. Copenhagen.

Cole, S., 2005. Applied Transport Economies: Policy, Management & Decision Making, 3rd ed. Kogan Page, London.

Collin-Lange, V., 2013. Socialities in motion: automobility and car cruising in Iceland. Mobilities 8, 406–423.

Conley, J., McLaren, A.T., 2012. Car Troubles: Critical Studies of Automobility and Auto-Mobility. Ashgate, Farnham.

Copenhagen Municipality, 2019. Copenhagen City of Cyclists.

Copenhagen Municipality, 2011. Good, Better, Best. Copenhagen.

Copenhagen Municipality, 2006. Nørrebrogade Program. Copenhagen.

Couldry, N., Hepp, A., 2017. The Mediated Construction of Reality. Polity, Cambridge and Malden.

Cresswell, T., 2006. On the Move: Mobility in the Modern Western World. Routledge, London.

da Silva, D.C., King, D.A., Lemar, S., 2020. Accessibility in practice: 20-minute city as a sustainability planning goal. Sustainability (Switzerland) 12. https://doi.org/10.3390/SU12010129

Danish Technical University, 2018. Transport Economic Unit Prices (Transportøkonomiske enhedspriser). Copenhagen.

Davis, M., 2010. Who will build the ark? New Left Review 29–45.

de Souza e Silva, A., Sheller, M., 2014. Mobility and Locative Media: Mobile Communication in Hybrid Spaces. Routledge, New York.

DeLanda, M., 2006. A New Philosophy of Society: Assemblage Theory and Social Complexity. Continuum, London and New York.

Delanty, G., 2003. Community (Key Ideas). Routledge, New York.

Dennis, K., Urry, J., 2009. After the Car. Polity, Cambridge.

Dewey, J., 1954. Public & Its Problems. Swallow Press, Ohio.

Drewes Nielsen, L., 2006. The methods and implication of action research, in: Aagaard Nielsen, K., Svensson, L. (Eds.), Action Research and Interactive Research. Shaker Publishing, Maastricht, pp. 89–115.

Durkheim, E., 1997. The Division of Labor in Society. Free Press, New York.

Eddington, R., 2006. The Eddington Transport Study: Main Report: Transport's Role in Sustaining the UK's Productivity and Competiveness. TSO, London.

Egemose, J., 2011. Towards Democratic Sustainable Development. Social Learning through Upstream Public Engagement.

Elliot, A., 2021. Reinvention, 2nd ed. Routledge, New York.

Elliot, A., 2016. Identity Troubles, 1st ed. Routledge, Oxon.

Eriksen, T.H., 2004. Røtter og Føtter – identitet i en omskiftelig tid. Aschehoug, Oslo.

Eriksen, T.H., 2001. Tyranny of the Moment: Fast and Slow Time in the Information Age. Pluto Press, London.

Essebo, M., Baeten, G., 2012. Contradictions of 'Sustainable Mobility' – the illogic of growth and the logic of myth. Tijdschrift voor Economische en Sociale Geografie 103, 555–565. https://doi.org/10.1111/j.1467-9663.2012.00733.x

European Environment Agency, 2018. Final energy consumption by mode of transport. (accessed 9.30.19).

Evers, A., Nowotny, H., 1987. Über den Umgang mit Unsicherheit [Broschiert]. Suhrkamp, Frankfurt/Main.

Fainstein, S.S., DeFilippis, J., 2016. Readings in Planning Theory, 4th ed. https://doi.org/10.1002/9781119084679

Fairclough, N., Jessop, B., Sayer, A., 2002. Critical realism and semiosis. Journal of Critical Realism 5, 2–10.

Fallov, M.A., Jørgensen, A., Knudsen, L.B., 2013. Mobile forms of belonging. Mobilities 8, 467–486. https://doi.org/10.1080/17450101.2013.769722

Featherstone, M., 2004. Automobilities: an introduction. Theory, Culture & Society 21, 1–24.

Fernández, X.L., Gundelfinger, J., Coto-Millán, P., 2021. The impact of logistics and intermodality on airport efficiency. Transport Policy. https://doi.org/10.1016/j.tranpol.2021.05.008

Fischer, F., Forester, J., 1993. The Argumentative Turn in Policy Analysis and Planning. Duke University Press, Durham.

Fischer, F., Gottweis, H., 2012. The argumentative turn revisited, in: Fischer, F., Gottweis, H. (Eds.), The Argumentative Turn Revisited. Duke University Press, Durham, pp. 1–27.

Fisher, E., 1979. Woman's Creation: Sexual Evolution and the Shaping of Society, 1st ed. Anchor Press/Doubleday, Garden City, New York.

Fjalland, E.L.P., 2019. Rebellious Waste and Food: Searching for Reparative Futures within Urban-Rural Landscapes.

Fjalland, E.L.P., 2018. A carrier bag story of (waste) food, hens and the sharing economy. Applied Mobilities 3, 34–50. https://doi.org/10.1080/23800127.201 8.1435439

Fraedrich, E., Lenz, B., 2014. Automated driving: individual and societal aspects entering the debate. Transportation Research Record: Journal of the Transportation Research Board. https://doi.org/10.3141/2416-08

Freudendal-Pedersen, M., 2021. Vélomobility in Copenhagen – a perfect world?, in: The Politics of Cycling Infrastructure. https://doi.org/10.46692/9781447345169.010

Freudendal-Pedersen, M., 2020. Sustainable urban futures from transportation and planning to networked urban mobilities. Transportation Research Part D: Transport and Environment. https://doi.org/10.1016/j.trd.2020.102310

Freudendal-Pedersen, M., 2018. Engaging with sustainable urban mobilities in Western Europe: urban utopias seen through cycling in Copenhagen, in: Low, S. (Ed.), The Routledge Handbook of Anthropology and the City. Routledge, New York and London, pp. 216–229.

Freudendal-Pedersen, M., 2015a. Cyclists as part of the city's organism – structural stories on cycling in Copenhagen. City & Society 27, 30–50.

Freudendal-Pedersen, M., 2015b. Whose commons are mobilities spaces? – The case of Copenhagen's cyclists. ACME 14, 598–621.

Freudendal-Pedersen, M., 2014a. Tracing the super rich and their mobilities in a scandinavian welfare state, in: Birtchnell, T., Caletío, J. (Eds.), Elite Mobilities. Routledge, London and New York, pp. 209–225.

Freudendal-Pedersen, M., 2014b. Searching for ethics and responsibilities of everyday life mobilities. Sociologica 8, 1–23.

Freudendal-Pedersen, M., 2009. Mobility in Daily Life: Between Freedom and Unfreedom. Ashgate, Farnham.

Freudendal-Pedersen, M., 2007. Mobility, motility and freedom the structural story as analytical tool for understanding the interconnection. Schweizerische Zeitschrift für Soziologie 33, 27–43.

Freudendal-Pedersen, M., 2005. Structural stories, mobility and (un)freedom, in: Thomsen, T.U., Drewes Nielsen, L., Gudmunson, A. (Eds.), Social Perspectives on Mobility. Ashgate, Aldershot, pp. 29–46.

Freudendal-Pedersen, M., Adey, P., Bissel, D., Hannam, K., Merriman, P., 2014. Ethics and responsibilities, in: Sheller, M. (Ed.), The Routledge Handbook of Mobilities. Routledge, London and New York, pp. 143–153.

Freudendal-Pedersen, M., Hannam, K., Kesselring, S., 2016. Applied mobilities, transitions and opportunities. Applied Mobilities 1, 1–9.

Freudendal-Pedersen, M., Hartmann-Petersen, K., Friis, F., Lindberg, M.R., Grindsted, T.S., 2020. Sustainable mobility in the mobile risk society-designing innovative mobility solutions in copenhagen. Sustainability (Switzerland) 12. https://doi.org/10.3390/su12177218

Freudendal-Pedersen, M., Hartmann-Petersen, K., Nielsen, L.D., 2010. Mixing methods in the search for mobile complexity, in: Fincham, B., McGuinness, M., Murray, L. (Eds.), Mobile Methodologies. Palgrave Macmillan, New York, pp. 25–43.

Freudendal-Pedersen, M., Kesselring, S., 2021. What is the urban without physical mobilities? COVID-19-induced immobility in the mobile risk society. Mobilities 16. https://doi.org/10.1080/17450101.2020.1846436

Freudendal-Pedersen, M., Kesselring, S., 2018a. Exploring Networked Urban Mobilities: Theories, Concepts, Ideas. Routledge, London and Chicago.

Freudendal-Pedersen, M., Kesselring, S., 2018b. Networked urban mobilities, in: Freudendal-Pedersen, M., Kesselring, S. (Eds.), Exploring Networked Urban Mobilities: Theories, Concepts, Ideas. Routledge, New York, pp. 1–19. https://doi.org/10.4324/9781315201078-1

Freudendal-Pedersen, M., Kesselring, S., 2018c. Sharing mobilities. Some propaedeutic considerations. Applied Mobilities 3. https://doi.org/10.1080/2380 0127.2018.1438235

Freudendal-Pedersen, M., Kesselring, S., 2016. Mobilities, futures and the city. Repositioning discourses – changing perspectives – rethinking policies. Mobilities 11, 573–584.

Freudendal-Pedersen, M., Kesselring, S., Servou, E., 2019. What is smart for the future city? Mobilities and Automation. Sustainability 11, 1–21. https://doi. org/, https://doi.org/10.3390/su11010221

Friedman, J., 2011. Insurgencies: Essays in Planning Theory. Routledge, Abingdon.

Friedman, J., 2002. The Prospects of Cities. University of Minnesota Press, Minneapolis.

Friedmann, J., 1987. Planning in the Public Domain, 1st ed. Princeton University Press, Princeton. https://doi.org/10.2307/j.ctv10crf8d

Galland, D., Tewdwr-Jones, M., 2019. Past, present, future: the historical evolution of metropolitan planning conceptions and styles, in: Metropolitan Regions, Planning and Governance. https://doi.org/10.1007/978-3-030-25632-6_11

Gehl Architects, 2005. Byrum og Byliv Nørrebrogade. Copenhagen.

Gehl, J., 2011. Life Between Buildings: Using Public Space, Disciplina_Fabio.

Geurs, K.T., van Wee, B., 2004. Accessibility evaluation of land-use and transport strategies: review and research directions. Journal of Transport Geography 12. https://doi.org/10.1016/j.jtrangeo.2003.10.005

Giddens, A., 1991. Modernity and Self-Identity: Self and Society in the Late Modern Age. Stanford University Press, Stanford.

Giddens, A., 1984. The Constitution of Society: Outline of the Theory of Structuration. University of California Press, Berkeley.

Giddens, P.A., 2002. Runaway World. Profile Books, London.

Glaveanu, V.P., Womersley, G., 2021. Affective mobilities: migration, emotion and (im)possibility. Mobilities. https://doi.org/10.1080/17450101.2021.1920337

Goffman, E., 1959. The Presentation of Self in Everyday Life. University of Edinburgh Social Sciences Research Center, Edinburgh, UK, Doubleday, New York.

Goffman, I., 1971. Relations in Public: Microstudies of the Public Order. Basic Books, New York.

Goletz, M., Haustein, S., Wolking, C., L'Hostis, A., 2020. Intermodality in European metropolises: the current state of the art, and the results of an expert survey covering Berlin, Copenhagen, Hamburg and Paris. Transport Policy 94. https://doi.org/10.1016/j.tranpol.2020.04.011

Graham, S., Marvin, S., 2002. Splintering Urbanism, Networked Infrastructures, Technological Mobilities and the Urban Condition, 1st ed. Taylor & Francis, London.

Guillaume, X., Huysmans, J., 2019. The concept of 'the everyday': ephemeral politics and the abundance of life. Cooperation and Conflict 54. https://doi.org/10.1177/0010836718815520

Hägerstraand, T., 1970. What about people in Regional Science? Papers in Regional Science. https://doi.org/10.1111/j.1435-5597.1970.tb01464.x

Hajer, M., 2017. The Power of Imagination. Inaugural Lecture on the Occasion of the Acceptance of the Distinguished Professorship in 'Urban Futures.'

Hajer, M., 2016. On being smart about cities: seven considerations for a new urban planning and design, in: Allen, A., Lampis, A., Swilling, M. (Eds.), Untamed Urbanism. Routledge, Oxon, New York, pp. 50–63.

Hajer, M., 1999. Zero-Friction Society. https://www.rudi.net/books/11454 (accessed 5.29.14).

Hajer, M., Versteeg, W., 2019. Imagining the post-fossil city: why is it so difficult to think of new possible worlds? Territory, Politics, Governance. https://doi.org/10.1080/21622671.2018.1510339

Hajer, M.A., Pelzer, P., 2018. 2050—An energetic Odyssey: understanding 'Techniques of Futuring' in the transition towards renewable energy. Energy Research and Social Science. https://doi.org/10.1016/j.erss.2018.01.013

Halkier, B., 2010. Focus groups as social enactments: integrating interaction and content in the analysis of focus group data. Qualitative Research 10, 71–89.

Hannam, K., 2016. Tourism, mobilities and the geopolitics of erasure, in: Hall, D. (Ed.), Tourism and Geopolitics. CABI, Wallingford.

Hannam, K., Sheller, M., Urry, J., 2006. Editorial: mobilities, immobilities and moorings. Mobilities 1, 1–22.

Hanson, S., 1995. The Geography of Urban Transportation, 2nd ed.

Haraway, D., 2016. Staying with the Trouble: Making Kin in the Chtlucene. Chicago Manual Press, Chicago.

Hartmann-Petersen, K., 2020. Providing and working in rhythms, in: Jensen, O.B., Lassen, C., Kaufmann, V., Freudendal-Pedersen, M., Lange, I.S.G. (Eds.), Routledge Handbook of Urban Mobilities. Routledge, Oxon, New York.

Harvey, D., 2001. Globalization and the "Spatial Fix.". Geographische Revue 2, 22–30.

Harvey, D., 2000. Spaces of Hope. Edinburgh University Press, Edinburgh.

Healey, P., 1997. Collaborative Planning. UBC Press, Vancouver.

Heinlein, M., Kropp, C., Neumer, J., Poferl, A., Römhild, R., 2012. Futures of Modernity. Challenges for Cosmopolitical Thought and Practice. Transcript (Sociology), Bielefeld.

Heller, A., 1995. Where are we at home? Thesis Eleven 41, 1–18.

High-level Advisory Group on Sustainable Transport, 2016. Mobilizing Sustainable Transport for Development. New York.

Hollands, R.G., 2014. Critical interventions into the corporate smart city. Cambridge Journal of Regions, Economy and Society 8, 61–77.

Howard, E., 1902. Garden Cities of Tomorrow, Organization & Environment. Swan Sonnenschein & Company, Limited.

Hughes, A., Mee, K., 2019. Co-mobility in the digital age: changing technologies, and the affects of presence in journeying 'with' others. Applied Mobilities. https://doi.org/10.1080/23800127.2019.1607425

Ingold, T., 2007. Lines: A Brief History. Routledge, Oxon, New York.

Jacobs, J., 1961. The death and life of great American cities, in: The Failure of Town Planning. New York. https://doi.org/10.2307/794509

Jensen, H.L., 2012. Emotions on the move: mobile emotions among train commuters in the South East of Denmark. Emotion, Space and Society 5, 201–206.

Jensen, O.B., 2021. Pandemic disruption, extended bodies, and elastic situations – reflections on COVID-19 and mobilities. Mobilities 16. https://doi.org/10.1080/17450101.2021.1867296

Jensen, O.B., 2014. Designing Mobilities. Aalborg Universitetsforlag, Aalborg.

Jensen, O.B., 2013. Staging Mobilities (International Library of Sociology). Routledge, London.

Jensen, O.B., 2010. Erving goffman and everyday life mobility, in: Jacobsen, M.H. (Ed.), The Contemporary Goffman. Routledge, New York, pp. 333–351.

Jensen, O.B., 2009. Flows of meaning, cultures of movements – urban mobility as meaningful everyday life practice. Mobilities 4, 139–158.

Jensen, O.B., 2006. 'Facework', flow and the city: Simmel, Goffman, and mobility in the contemporary city. Mobilities 1. https://doi.org/10.1080/17450100600726506

Jensen, O.B., Freudendal-Pedersen, M., 2012. Utopias of mobilities, in: Jacobsen, M.H., Tester, K. (Eds.), Utopia: Social Theory and the Future. Ashgate, Farnham, pp. 197–218.

Jensen, O.B., Lassen, C., Kaufmann, V., Freudendal-Pedersen, M., Lange, I.S.G., 2020. Routledge Handbook of Urban Mobilities. Routledge Taylor & Francis Group, London and New York.

Jensen, O.B., Lassen, C., Lange, I.S.G., 2019. Material Mobilities. Routledge, New York.

Jensen, O.B., Richardson, T., 2003. Making European Space: Mobility, Power and Territorial Identity. Routledge, London.

Johansen, A.G., 2021. Opaqueness and tangibility: a post-ANT account of the operationalisation of liveability in strategic planning. The city of Copenhagen, 2017–2020. Copenhagen.

Jorgensen, A., 2010a. The sense of belonging in new urban zones of transition. Current Sociology 58, 3–23.

Jorgensen, A., 2010b. The sense of belonging in new urban zones of transition. Current Sociology. https://doi.org/10.1177/0011392109348542

Jungk, R., Müllert, N., 1987. Future Workshops: How to Create Desirable Futures. Institute for Social Inventions, London.

Juul, S., 2002. Modernitet, velfærd og solidaritet: en undersøgelse af danskernes moralske forpligtelser [Modernity, Welfare and Solidarity: An Investigation on Danes' Moral Obligations]. Hans Reitzel, Copenhagen.

Kaplan, A., Ross, K., 1987. Everyday Life, Yale French Studies. Yale University Press, New Haven.

Kaufmann, V., 2011. ReThinking the City (Urbanism). Routledge, Oxford.

Kaufmann, V., 2002. Re-Thinking Mobility: Contemporary Sociology (Transport and Society). Ashgate, Oxford.

Kaufmann, V., Bergman, M.M., Joye, D., 2004. Motility: mobility as capital. International Journal of Urban and Regional Research 28. https://doi.org/10.1111/j.0309-1317.2004.00549.x

Kelly, T., 2001. The Art of Innovation: Lessons in Creativity from IDEO, America's Leading Design Firm. Currency Books, New York.

Kemp, R., Martens, P., 2007. Sustainable development: how to manage something that is subjective and never can be achieved? Sustainable Development 3, 5–14.

Kesselring, S., 2019. Reflexive Mobilitäten, in: Pelizäus, H., Nieder, L. (Eds.), Das Risiko – Gedanken Übers Und Ins Ungewisse. Interdisziplinäre Aushandlungen Des Risikophänomens Im Lichte Der Reflexiven Moderne. Eine Festschrift Für Wolfgang Bonß. Springer VS, Wiesbaden, pp. 165–204.

Kesselring, S., 2009. Global transfer points: the making of airports in the mobile risk society, in: Cwerner, S., Kesselring, S., Urry, J. (Eds.), Aeromobilities, International Library of Sociology. Routledge, London and New York, pp. 39–60.

Kesselring, S., 2008a. The mobile risk society, in: Kesselring, S., Kaufmann, V., Weert, C. (Eds.), Tracing Mobilities. Ashgate, Aldershot, pp. 77–104.

Kesselring, S., 2008b. Scating over thin ice. Pioneers of the mobile risk society, in: Pflieger, G., Pattaroni, L., Jemelin, C., Kaufmann, V. (Eds.), The Social Fabric of the Networked City. EPFL Press, Lausanne, pp. 17–39.

Kesselring, S., 2006. Pioneering mobilities: new patterns of movement and motility in a mobile world. Environment and Planning A 38, 269–279.

Kesselring, S., Freudendal-Pedersen, M., 2021. Searching for urban mobilities futures. Methodological innovation in the light of COVID-19. Sustainable Cities and Society.

Kesselring, S., Freudendal-Pedersen, M., Zuev, D., 2020. Sharing mobilities and the mobile risk society, in: Sharing Mobilities. https://doi.org/10.4324/9780429489242-1

Kesselring, S., Vogl, G., 2008. Networks, scapes and flows – mobility pioneers between first and second modernity, in: Canzler, W., Kaufmann, V., Kesselring, S. (Eds.), Tracing Mobilities. Ashgate, Aldershot and Burlington, pp. 163–180.

Kitchin, R., 2015. Making sense of smart cities: addressing present shortcomings. Cambridge Journal of Regions, Economy and Society 8, 131–136. https://doi.org/10.1093/cjres/rsu027

Kitchin, R., Dodge, M., 2009. Aiport code/spaces, in: Cwerner, S., Kesselring, S., Urry, J. (Eds.), Aeromobilities, International Library of Sociology. Routledge, London and New York, pp. 96–114.

Koglin, T., 2013. Vélomobility – A critical analysis of planning and space. PhD.

Krasheninnikov, A. v., 2019. Accessibility and connectivity as the key factors of the macro-space in built environment. Civil Engineering and Architecture 7. https://doi.org/10.13189/cea.2019.070201

Kurth, M., Kozlowski, W., Ganin, A., Mersky, A., Leung, B., Dykes, J., Kitsak, M., Linkov, I., 2020. Lack of resilience in transportation networks: economic implications. Transportation Research Part D: Transport and Environment 86. https://doi.org/10.1016/j.trd.2020.102419

Kvale, S., 1996. InterViews: An Introduction to Qualitative Research Interviewing. SAGE, London.

Kvale, S., Brinkmann, S., 2009. InterView: Introduktion til et håndværk, 2. udgave. ed. Hans Reitzels Forlag, Copenhagen.

Lan, Z., Cai, M., 2021. Dynamic traffic noise maps based on noise monitoring and traffic speed data. Transportation Research Part D: Transport and Environment 94. https://doi.org/10.1016/j.trd.2021.102796

Larner, W., 2000. Neoliberalism: policy, ideology, governmentality. Studies in Political Economy 63, 5–25.

Larsen, J., Axhausen, J.U., Urry, K., 2006. Mobilities, Networks, Geographies. Ashgate, Aldershot.

Latour, B., 1991. Technology is society made durable, in: A Sociology of Monsters: Essays on Power, Technology and Domination. https://doi.org/citeulike-article-id:3331003

Laurier, E., Lorimer, H., Brown, B., Jones, O., Juhlin, O., Noble, A., Perry, M., Pica, D., Sormani, P., Strebel, I., Swan, L., Taylor, A., Watts, L., Weilenmann, A., 2008. Driving and "passengering": notes on the ordinary organization of car travel. Mobilities 3. https://doi.org/10.1080/17450100701797273

le Corbusier, 1947. The Four Routes. Dennis Dobson, London.

Lefebvre, H., 2003. The Urban Revolution. University of Minnesota Press, Minneapolis.

Lefebvre, H., 1996. Writings on Cities. Blackwell Publishers, Malden.

Lefebvre, H., 1991a. Critique of Everyday Life I. Verso, London and New York. https://doi.org/10.1007/s13398-014-0173-7.2

Lefebvre, H., 1991b. The Production of Space. Blackwell, Oxford.

Lefebvre, H., 1984. Everyday Life in the Modern World. Transaction Books, Piscataway, NJ.

Lefebvre, H., 1976. The Survival of Capitalism. Allison and Busby, London.

Levitas, R., 2013. Utopia as Method: The Imaginary Reconstitution of Society. https://doi.org/10.1057/9781137314253

Licoppe, C., 2018. Mobile 'Pseudonymous strangers,' in: Exploring Networked Urban Mobilities. https://doi.org/10.4324/9781315201078-3

Licoppe, C., 2016. Mobilities and urban encounters in public places in the age of locative media. Seams, folds, and encounters with 'pseudonymous strangers.' Mobilities 11. https://doi.org/10.1080/17450101.2015.1097035

Licoppe, C., Inada, Y., 2010. Locative media and cultures of mediated proximity: the case of the mogi game location-aware community. Environment and Planning D: Society and Space 28. https://doi.org/10.1068/d13307

Light, A., Miskelly, C., 2015. Sharing economy vs sharing cultures? Designing for social, economic and environmental good. Interaction Design and Architecture(s).

Lippmann, W., 1993. The Phantom Public (International Organizations Series). Transaction Publishers, Piscataway, NJ.

Listerborn, C., Neergaard, M., 2021. Uncovering the "Cracks"? Bringing feminist urban research into smart city research. ACME 20, 294–311.

Litman, T., 2006. London Congestion Pricing.

Lofland, L., 1998. The Public Realm: Exploring the City's Quintessential Social Territory. Routledge, London and New York.

Lydon, M., Garcia, A., 2015. Tactical Urbanism: Short-Term Action for Long-Term Change. Island Press, Washington, DC.

Lyubomirsky, S., Sheldon, K.M., Schkade, D., 2005. Pursuing happiness: the architecture of sustainable change. Review of General Psychology. https://doi.org/10.1037/1089-2680.9.2.111

Martin, C.J., 2015. The sharing economy: a pathway to sustainability or a new nightmarish form of neoliberalism? Ecological Economics 121, 149–159.

Martin, R., 2021a. Points of Exchange: Spatial Strategies for the Transition Towards Sustainable Urban Mobilities. Copenhagen.

Martin, R., 2021b. Ontological expansion through the visualisation of space: an architect's contribution to the sustainable urban mobilities agenda. Applied Mobilities.

Marx, K., 1976. Capital. Volume 1. Penguin, London.

Mason, P., 2016. PostCapitalism: A Guide to Our Future. Penguin, London.

Massey, D., 2005. For Space. SAGE, London.

Mattauch, L., Ridgway, M., Creutzig, F., 2016. Happy or liberal? Making sense of behavior in transport policy design. Transportation Research Part D: Transport and Environment 45, 64–83.

Mell, I., Whitten, M., 2021. Access to nature in a post covid-19 world: opportunities for green infrastructure financing, distribution and equitability in urban planning. International Journal of Environmental Research and Public Health. https://doi.org/10.3390/ijerph18041527

Mikulak, M., 2013. The Politics of the Pantry: Stories, Food, and Social Change. McGill-Queen's University Press, Montreal.

Moreno-garcia, M.C., 1994. Intensity and form of the urban heat island in Barcelona. International Journal of Climatology 14. https://doi.org/10.1002/joc.3370140609

Munford, L.A., 2017. The impact of congestion charging on social capital. Transportation Research Part A: Policy and Practice 97. https://doi.org/10.1016/j.tra.2017.01.018

Næss, P., Andersen, J., Nicolaisen, M.S., Strand, A., 2014. Transport modelling in the context of the "predict and provide" paradigm. European Journal of Transport and Infrastructure Research 14. https://doi.org/10.18757/ejtir.2014.14.2.3020

Newman, P., Kenworthy, J.R., 2015. The End of Automobile Dependence. Island, Washington, DC.

Nielsen, B.S., Nielsen, K.A., 2006. Methodologies in action research, in: Nielsen, K.A., Svensson, L. (Eds.), Action Research and Interactive Research Beyond Practice and Theory. Shaker publishing, Maastricht, pp. 63–87.

Nixon, D., 2012. A sense of momentum: mobility practices and dis/embodied landscapes of energy use. Environment and Planning A 44, 1661–1678.

Notar, B.E., 2012. Coming Out' to 'Hit the Road': temporal, spatial and affective mobilities of taxi drivers and day trippers in Kunming. China. City & Society 24, 281–301.

Nowotny, H., Scott, P., Gibbons, M., 2001. Re-Thinking Science: Knowledge and the Public in an Age of Uncertainty. Polity, Cambridge.

Obrador-Pons, P., Crang, M., Travlou, P., 2009. Cultures of Mass Tourism: Doing the Mediterranean in the Ae of Banal Mobilities. New Directions in Tourism Analysis. Ashgate, Farnham.

Ostrom, E., 2012. The Future of the Commons. Profile Books, London.

Pearce, L., 2016. Drivetime: Literary Excursions in Automotive Consciousness. Edinburgh University Press, Edinburgh.

Peñalosa, E., 2008. Politics, power, cities', in: Burdett, R., Sudjic, D. (Eds.), The Endless City. Phaidon Press, London.

Philips, I., Anable, J., Chatterton, T., 2020. E-bike carbon savings – how much and where? Oxford.

Picard, D., Buchberger, S., 2013. Couchsurfing Cosmopolitanisms. Can Tourism Make a Better World? Transcript-Verlag, Bielefeld.

Pinder, D., 2020. Situationism/Situationist City, in: International Encyclopedia of Human Geography. https://doi.org/10.1016/b978-0-08-102295-5.10700-0

Pinder, D., 2005. Visions of the City: Utopianism, Power and Politics in Twentieth-Century Urbanism. Edinburgh University Press, Edinburgh.

Plant, S., 2002. The Most Radical Gesture. https://doi.org/10.4324/9780203210260

Pooley, C.G., Turnbull, J., Adams, M., 2006. A Mobile Century?: Changes in Everyday Mobility in Britain in the Twentieth Century (Transport and Mobility). Ashgate, Aldershot.

Pucci, P., Vecchio, G., 2019. Enabling Mobilities: Planning Tools for People and Their Mobilities. Springer, Sham.

Putnam, R.D., 2000. Bowling Alone: The Collapse and Revival of American Community. Touchstone Books by Simon & Schuster, New York.

Rahimi, M., Hakimpour, F., 2018. An integrated framework based on cloud computing for map matching analysis of floating car data. Journal of Geomatics Science and Technology 7.

Rainie, H., Wellman, B., 2012. Networked: the New Social Operating System. MIT Press, Cambridge, MA.

Reckwitz, A., 2002. Toward a theory of social practices: a development in culturalist theorizing. European Journal of Social Theory 5. https://doi.org/10.1177/13684310222225432

Redclift, M., 1992. The meaning of sustainable development. Geoforum 25, 395–403. https://doi.org/10.1016/0016-7185(92)90050-E

Rheingold, H., 1994. The virtual community. Secker & Warburg, London.

Richardson, L., 2015. Performing the sharing economy. Geoforum. https://doi.org/10.1016/j.geoforum.2015.11.004

Rifkin, J., 2014. The Zero Marginal Cost Society – the Internet of Things, the Collaborative Commons, and the Eclipse of Capitalism. St. Martin's Press, New York.

Rifkin, J., 2000. The Age of Access: the New culture of Hypercapitalism, Where All of Life Is a Paid-For Experience. J.P. Tarcher/Putnam, New York.

Ritzer, G., 2010. Globalization: A Basic Text. Wiley-Blackwell, Oxford.

Rochet, C., 2018. Smart Cities: Reality or Fiction. Wiley, London and Hoboken.

Rode, P., Hoffmann, C., Kandt, J., Smith, D., Graff, A., 2015. Towards New Urban Mobility: The Case of London and Berlin. LSE Cities, London.

Rosaldo, R., 1989. Culture and Truth: the remaking of social analysis. Beacon Press, Boston.

Sachs, W., 1993. Global Ecology: A New Arena of Political Conflict. Zed Books, London.

Sachs, W., Tilman, S., Patrick, C., 2007. Fair Future: Resource Conflicts, Security and Global Justice: A Report of the Wuppertal Institute for Climate, Environment and Energy. Zed Books, London.

Sadler, S., 1999. The Situationist City. MIT Press, Boston.

Sadler, S., 1998. The Situationist City. MIT Press, Cambridge.

Salazar, N.B., 2021. Existential vs. essential mobilities: insights from before, during and after a crisis. Mobilities 16. https://doi.org/10.1080/17450101.2020.1866320

Sandercock, L., 2003. Out of the closet: the importance of stories and storytelling in planning practice. Planning Theory Practice 4, 11–28.

Savage, M., Bagnall, G., Longhurst, B., 2005. Globalization and Belonging. https://doi.org/10.4135/9781446216880

Sayer, A., 2011. Why Things Matter to People: Social Science, Values and Ethical Life. Cambridge University Press, Cambridge.

Sayer, A., 2005. The Moral Significance of Class. Cambridge University Press, Cambridge.

Schatzki, T.R., Cetina, K.K., von Savigny, E., 2005. The Practice Turn in Contemporary Theory. https://doi.org/10.4324/9780203977453

Schmalz-Bruns, R., 1995. Reflexive Demokratie. Nomos Verl.-Ges, Baden-Baden.

Schor, J.B., Attwood-Charles, W., 2017. The "sharing" economy: labor, inequality, and social connection on for-profit platforms. Wiley Sociology Compass. https://doi.org/https://doi.org/10.1111/soc4.12493

Sennett, R., 2007. The Open City, in: Burdett, R., Sudjic, D. (Eds.), The Endless City. Phaidon Press, London, pp. 290–297.

Sennett, R., 2003. Respect in a World of Inequality. W. W. Norton & Company, New York.

Sennett, R., 1977. The Fall of Public Man. Cambridge University Press, Cambridge.

Sharifi, F., Birt, A.G., Gu, C., Shelton, J., Farzaneh, R., Zietsman, J., Fraser, A., Chester, M., 2021. Regional CO_2 impact assessment of road infrastructure improvements. Transportation Research Part D: Transport and Environment 90. https://doi.org/10.1016/j.trd.2020.102638

Sheller, M., 2018. Mobility Justice: The Politics of Movement in an Age of Extremes. Verso, London.

Sheller, M., 2004. Automotive emotions: feeling the car. Theory, Culture & Society 21, 221–242.

Sheller, M., Urry, J., 2016. Mobilizing the new mobilities paradigm. Applied Mobilities 1, 10–25. https://doi.org/10.1080/23800127.2016.1151216

Sheller, M., Urry, J., 2006. The new mobilities paradigm. Environment and Planning A 38, 207–226.

Shiva, V., 2016. Earth Democracy: Justice, Sustainability and Peace, 2nd ed. Zed Books Ltd., London.

Shove, E., Pantzar, M., Watson, M., 2012. The dynamics of social practice, in: The Dynamics of Social Practice: Everyday Life and How It Changes. pp. 1–19. https://doi.org/10.4135/9781446250655.n1

Shove, E., Walker, G., 2010. Governing transitions in the sustainability of everyday life. Research Policy 39, 471–476.

Simmel, G., 1972. Georg Simmel on Individuality and Social Forms (Heritage of Sociology Series). University of Chicago Press, Chicago.

Simmel, G., 1971. Metropolis and mental life, in: Georg Simmel on Individuality and Social Forms: Selected Writings, pp. 324–339.

Spinney, J., 2020. Understanding Urban Cycling. https://doi.org/10.4324/9781351007122

Spinney, J., 2016. Fixing mobility in the neoliberal city: cycling policy and practice in London as a mode of political–economic and biopolitical governance. Annals of the American Association of Geographers. https://doi.org/10.1080/24694452.2015.1124016

Spinney, J., 2010. Improvising rhythms: re-reading urban time and space through everyday practices of cycling, in: Edensor, T. (Ed.), Geographies of Rhythm: Nature, Place, Mobility and Bodies. Ashgate, Farnham.

Spinney, J., 2007. Cycling the city: non-place and the sensory construction of meaning in a mobile place, in: Horton, D., Cox, P., Rosen, P. (Eds.), Cycling and Society. Ashgate, Hampshire.

Spurling, N., McMeekin, A., Shove, E., Southerton, D., Welch, D., 2013. Interventions in practice: Re-framing policy approaches to consumer behaviour.

Steel, C., 2008. Hungry City: How Food Shapes Our Lifes. Vintage Books, London.

Stephany, A., 2015. The Business of Sharing, The Business of Sharing. Palgrave Macmillan, New York. https://doi.org/10.1057/9781137376183

Sudjic, D., 2007. Theory, policy and pratice, in: Burdett, R., Sudjic, D. (Eds.), The Endless City. Phaidon Press, London and New York, pp. 32–51.

Swyngedouw, E., 2010. Apocalypse forever?: Post-political populism and the spectre of climate change. Theory, Culture & Society 27, 213–232.

Tarr, J., 1989. Infrastructure and city-building in the nineteenth and twentieth centuries, in: Haysa, S.P. (Ed.), City at the Point: Essays on the Social History of Pittsburgh. University of Pittsburgh Press, Pittsburgh, pp. 213–264.

Taylor, Z., Hoyle, B., Knowles, R., 2001. Modern transport geography. Economic Geography 77. https://doi.org/10.2307/3594099

Thomsen, T.U., 2005. Parents' construction of traffic safety: Children's independent mobility at risk? in: Thomsen, T.U., Drewes Nielsen, L., Gudmundsson, H. (Eds.), Social Perspectives On Mobility (Transport and Society). Ashgate, Aldershot, pp. 11–28.

Thrift, N., 2004. Driving in the city. Theory, Culture & Society 21, 41–59.

Thrift, N., 2001. "Still life in nearly present time: the object of nature,", in: Macnaghten, P., Urry, J. (Eds.), Bodies of Nature. SAGE, London, pp. 34–57.

Throgmorton, J., 2003. Planning as persuasive storytelling in a global-scale web of relationships. Planning Theory 2, 125–151.

Tickell, A., Peck, J., 2002. Neoliberalizing space. Antipode 34, 380–404. https://doi.org/DOI: 10.1111/1467-8330.00247

Tonboe, J., 1993. Rummets Sociologi: Kritik af teoretiseringen af den materielle omverdens betydning i den sociologiske og den kulturgeografiske tradition. Akademisk Forlag, København.

Tönnies, F., 1957. Community and Society. Courier Dover Publications, Mineola, New York.

Trafikministeriet, 2000. Hundrede års trafik. København.

Tsing, A., 2009. Supply chains and the human condition. Rethinking Marxism 21, 148–176.

Tyfield, D., 2018. Liberalism 2.0 and the Rise of China Global Crisis and Innovation. Routledge, London.

Urry, J., 2016. What Is the Future? Polity, Cambridge, UK & Malden, MA.

Urry, J., 2007. Mobilities. Polity, Cambridge.

Urry, J., 2006. Inhabiting the car. The Sociological Review 54, 17–31. https://doi.org/10.1111/j.1467-954X.2006.00635.x

Urry, J., 2004. The "system" of automobility. Theory, Culture & Society 21, 25–39.

Urry, J., 2000. Sociology Beyond Societies: Mobilities for the Twenty-First Century. Routledge, London and New York.

Vergragt, P.J., Brown, H.S., 2007. Sustainable mobility: from technological innovation to societal learning. Journal of Cleaner Production. https://doi.org/10.1016/j.jclepro.2006.05.020

Viba, A., 2014. The rise of collaborative consumption: a critical assessment of resistance to capitalism and its ideologies of self and property.

Virilio, P., 1998. Cyberworld: Det værstes politik. Introite, Frederiksberg.

von Essen, H., van Grinsven, A., Aalberts-Bakker, J., Skinner, I., 2018. Green Light for Sustainable Mobility: Vision and Pathway to 2050. Delft.

Wagner, L., 2018. Viscosities and meshwork, in: Experiencing Networked Urban Mobilities. https://doi.org/10.4324/9781315200255-11

Walker, L., Figliozzi, M.A., Haire, A.R., MacArthur, J., 2011. Identifying surface transportation vulnerabilities and risk assessment opportunities under climate change: case study in Portland, Oregon. Transportation Research Record. https://doi.org/10.3141/2244-06

Wang, T., Qu, Z., Yang, Z., Nichol, T., Clarke, G., Ge, Y.E., 2020. Climate change research on transportation systems: climate risks, adaptation and planning. Transportation Research Part D: Transport and Environment 88. https://doi.org/10.1016/j.trd.2020.102553

Wasserman, S., Faust, K., 1994. Social Network Analysis : Methods and Applications. Cambridge University Press, Cambridge.

Weber, M., 1978. Economy and Society: An Outline of Interpretive Sociology, Band 1. University of California Press, Berkeley.

Weber, M., 1949. The Methodology of the Social Sciences. The Free Press of Glencoe, Glencoe, IL.

Weliwitiya, H., Rose, G., Johnson, M., 2019. Bicycle train intermodality: effects of demography, station characteristics and the built environment. Journal of Transport Geography 74. https://doi.org/10.1016/j.jtrangeo.2018.12.016

Wellman, B., 2001. Computer networks as social networks. Science. https://doi.org/10.1126/science.1065547

Wellman, B., 1999. Networks in the Global Village. https://doi.org/10.4324/9780429498718

Wellman, B., Gulia, M., 1999. Virtual communities as communities: net surfers don't ride alone, in: Smith, M.A., Kollock, P. (Eds.), Communities in Cyberspace. Routledge, London, pp. 167–194.

Wilken, R., 2010. A community of strangers? Mobile media, art, tactility and urban encounters with the other. Mobilities 5, 449–468.

Wolf, W., 1996. Car Mania: A Critical History of Transport, 1770–1990. Pluto Press, Chicago.

World Business Counsil for Sustainable Development, 2004. Mobility 2030: Meeting the Challenges to Sustainability. Conches, Geneva.

Zeitler, U., 2008. The ontology of mobility, morality and transport planning, in: Bergmann, S., Sager, T. (Eds.), The Ethics of Mobilities: Rethinking Place, Exclusion, Freedom and Environment. Ashgate, Farnham, pp. 233–240.

Zeitler, U., 1998. Mobilitet og moral – aspekter af en transportetik.

Index

For Product Safety Concerns and Information please contact our EU
representative GPSR@taylorandfrancis.com
Taylor & Francis Verlag GmbH, Kaufingerstraße 24, 80331 München, Germany